Award-Winning

Wood Boxes

■■■■■■■■■■■■■■■■■■■■■■■■■■■■■■

11/96

Award-Winning

Wood Boxes

DESIGN & TECHNIQUE

Tony Lydgate

Sterling Publishing Co., Inc. New York
A STERLING/CHAPELLE BOOK

Library of Congress Cataloging-in-Publication Data
Lydgate, Tony.
        Award-winning wood boxes : design & technique / Tony Lydgate.
            p. cm.
        "A Sterling / Chapelle book."
        Includes index.
        ISBN 0-8069-8841-X
        1. Woodwork.   2. Wooden boxes.   I. Title.
    TT200.L94 1994   94-48062
        745.593—dc20   CIP

10 9 8 7 6 5 4 3 2 1

A Sterling / Chapelle Book

Published by Sterling Publishing Company, Inc.
387 Park Avenue South
New York, NY 10016

Copyright © 1995 by
Chapelle Ltd.

Distributed in Canada by Sterling Publishing
c/o Canadian Manda Group
One Atlantic Avenue
Suite 105
Toronto, Ontario, Canada M6K 3E7

Distributed in Great Britain and Europe by Cassell PLC
Wellington House
125 Strand
London WC2R 0BB, England

Distributed in Australia by Capricorn Link (Australia) Pty Ltd.
P.O. Box 6651
Baulkham Hills, Business Centre, NSW 2153, Australia

Printed in Hong Kong.

Sterling ISBN 0-8069-8841-X

ACKNOWLEDGMENTS

RESEARCH, TEXT, AND ARTIST COORDINATION:

Tony Lydgate

ARTIST FOR DIAGRAMS:

Graham Blackburn

CONCEPT, DESIGN, AND PRODUCTION:

Chapelle Designers

Jo Packham, Owner

Cathy Sexton, Editor

PHOTOGRAPHY:

Kevin Dilley

for Hazen Photography

INTRODUCTION

By Tony Lydgate

The box is among the most common of everyday objects. Despite its familiarity, however, it holds a special fascination, because it conceals what it contains. The very fact that the contents are hidden from view makes them seem all the more desirable, and in this way the box creates a sense of allure and mystery.

The box is an ideal woodworking project because it is at heart a simple object, as well as one with a thousand uses. In this book, America's leading boxmakers present forty of their best designs. How-to building instructions, including exploded diagrams, invite woodworkers at any skill level, from beginner to master, to share the enjoyment of boxmaking. Most important, the book will not only help you get started in boxmaking, but it will inspire you to discover the art of the wood box by developing your own designs and exploring your own vision.

All projects are designed to be made in the home workshop, and are intended solely for personal use, and not for commercial manufacture or sale. The following pages offer an introduction to both the why and the how of boxmaking. Beginners may benefit from explanations of some of the tricks of the trade; the skilled will enjoy seeing which of their many secrets are explained, and which are left to be discovered.

1
Getting Started

A basic rule for success in boxmaking is to start where you are, with the tools you have available, and make a box — any box. Then make another box. Keep this up, and in time, looking back at your first efforts will become pleasantly embarrassing. When woodworking magazines and tool catalogs arrive in the mail, filled with their fabulous machinery and shiny gadgets, remember that up until quite recently, the great masters had no electric tools, no carbide bits, no aluminum oxide abrasives. Their masterpieces were created by persistently applying the very attributes you have in such abundance: determination, elbow grease, and a firm belief in your own way of doing things.

Whether making a box exactly as shown, using the plans as the basis for variations, or setting out to create something completely new, it is useful to start by visualizing the finished product. How does it fit the function it will serve? How well will its moveable parts operate, and how long will they last? Most important, enjoy imagining how great it will look, and how it will reflect the individual vision and style of its maker.

2
Tools

The right tools enable you to produce the best results in the most efficient manner. The many milling operations involved in boxmaking can be performed in different ways, including entirely by hand. The electric tools described below will help get the job done quicker and more easily.

Tablesaw

The boxmaker's basic tool, this machine will rip, crosscut, rabbet, resaw, dado, bevel, slot, trim, miter, and angle. A 10" blade diameter is the most practical, and heavier-duty models are preferable because they tend to be more accurate, especially for repeated cuts. A sturdy fence and adjustable miter fence are essential accessories. Saw blades should be carbide-tipped, and kept as sharp as possible. Kerf width, number and type of teeth vary according to the particular cut to be made. Blades accumulate resin, especially when milling dense hardwoods; after each hour of use, clean them with spray-on oven cleaner.

6" x 48" Belt Sander

Sanding objects with flat surfaces is easiest on a stationary belt sander, and 6" x 48" is a widely available and convenient size. Coarse grits such as 30x and 60x are useful for removing large areas of excess wood and/or glue. Medium-grit belts, 120x and 150x, shape, round, and bevel, and are essential intermediate steps in the overall sanding process. Polishing belts, described in more detail in Section 5, are the final stage in producing a perfect mirror finish.

The tablesaw and belt sander are the boxmaker's two workhorse tools. In ad-

dition, it is useful to own or have access to a drillpress, bandsaw, shaper (or router with router table), joiner, planer, thickness sander, and orbital or vibrator sander. These tools simplify many operations and save time. When one is not available, however, the skilled boxmaker will use ingenuity to develop an alternative technique, and this often leads to new designs and discoveries. In the perfectly equipped shop, where machines do most of the thinking, such serendipity is not so readily encountered.

Another source of serendipitous innovations is the errors that even the most skilled craftsman will inevitably make. It is said that the mark of a true master in any field is the ability to fix whatever mistakes arise; to this it should be added that a good boxmaker views a mistake not as a vexing obstacle, but rather as a creative opportunity.

3
What Woods
To Use

The secret to making great boxes is great wood.

Because of their relatively small size, boxes lend themselves to unique and unusual wood combinations. If supplies of a certain species are unobtainable, the best course is to substitute whatever is available. One often overlooked source for interesting woods is your own neighborhood: many of the native species that grow on our streets and in our backyards yield beautiful lumber. Moreover, grain patterns such as burl, birdseye, crotch, curly, or fiddleback appear in these species as frequently as in more familiar woods.

Whatever the species, boxmakers judge a piece of wood by color, grain, and especially the presence of figure. Nothing brings a box lid or drawer front alive like a small burl, knot, or flash of curl. When buying hardwoods from lumberyards, make sure any tropical species come from sources that practice sustainable yield forest management. And if the price of a board you covet seems high, weigh your cost-consciousness against the many hours of your painstaking labor that will go into fashioning the finished piece. Remember also that

9

that piece may well be among your descendants' prized possessions a century from now.

Many lumber dealers sell only pre-milled boards, with both faces planed and at least one edge ripped straight. This makes it easier to assess grain color and quality, but it also reduces available thickness: those piles of shavings on the sawmill floor are money, and surfaced lumber costs substantially more than the same lumber in the rough. Try to buy rough lumber whenever possible, and develop the ability to "read" the grain of rough-sawn boards. This permits detection of figure that a casual observer may miss, and also provides thicker stock to work with back in the shop.

Mixed Media: Using Unexpected Materials

Boxmakers have always used materials other than wood, such as brass for hinges and clasps, velvet or suede linings, glass and mirrors. As several of the designs in this book illustrate, contemporary boxmakers are increasingly incorporating materials as

10

diverse as tubular or sheet aluminum, driftwood, gold leaf, acrylic rod, found objects, vinyl tile, and slate. When used successfully, unconventional materials enhance the look of a box through contrast, allowing the boxmaker to reinterpret a traditional form in contemporary terms. What's more, using such materials makes available a host of colors and textures that do not occur in natural hardwood.

Swell and Shrink

Hardwood lumber was once a living material, and its pores breathe in response to the surrounding climate. Many an otherwise splendid box has been brought to grief by wood's natural tendency to shrink or swell, and experienced boxmakers use several approaches to cope with it.

First and most important, use only lumber that is properly kiln- or air-dried. Second, mill side walls and related parts thinner, rather than thicker. Where appropriate, utilize floating panels, in which the edges of a solid piece are milled with a keel to slide into kerfs or dadoes in the surrounding

frame. For massive parts, use finger joints, pins, dovetails, splines, slip feathers, or other types of joinery that provide a mechanical reinforcement for the adhesive bond.

Use veneers over a substrate of thin cross-grain laminates, most commonly known as plywood, wherever appropriate. Found in the tombs of the Egyptian Pharaohs, plywood is one of the most ancient of all woodworking innovations. Its dimensional stability is indispensible for spanning large areas. Veneer plywoods are used for the bottoms of many boxes and trays in this book because they are the best material for the job: strong, stable, and lightweight.

Despite all these precautions, remember that nothing is immune to the ravages of time. Finishes dull, colors fade, woods dry out, parts shift, adhesives weaken, and cracks open and close with the passing seasons. These do not detract from the beauty of a box — they just certify that it was made by a real person, using real materials.

4
Milling

From the simplest butt joint to the most complex dovetail, parts go together best — and stay together — only if they are properly milled to begin with. Once rough lumber for box parts has been selected and cut to rough size, each piece should be given a flat face, using the belt sander or joiner. (Because of their irregular grain, highly figured woods easily chip or tear out on the joiner, so use the belt sander for these.) With one side flat, parts can be accurately ripped to thickness. Add a hair to each final dimension to allow for finish sanding, and rip on the tablesaw using a push stick. If the finished piece is to be greater than about 3" tall, the maximum cutting height of a 10" table-saw blade, two passes will be needed to complete the rip cut to thickness.

Parts are then trimmed to width, again adding a hair to the dimension to allow for edge sanding. If available, an abrasive planer or thickness sander will make box parts uniform in dimension, and simplify the eventual finish-sanding process. Dimensioned and sanded parts are now ready for the slots, rabbets, dadoes, or holes that will later facilitate assembly of bottoms, rails, dowels, sides, and hinge pins.

Milling small pieces of wood can be awkward, and parts that will end up shorter than about 9" should be prepared "two up" whenever practical. Perform all dimensioning, slotting, and pre-assembly sanding operations on longer, easier-to-handle stock, and cross-cut to final size just prior to mitering.

In boxmaking, more than in any other type of woodworking, milling and assembly alternate in the sequence of fabrication steps leading to the final product. The dimensioned parts are glued together, and the resulting assembly is then re-milled in preparation for yet another assembly: this back-and-forth process may be repeated several times.

The Miter Joint

The miter is one of the most versatile means of joining box parts. The resulting joint is neat-looking, does not show end grain, and can be reinforced with splines or slip feathers. The secret to successful miters is accurate milling: make sure the angles of both the saw blade and the miter fence are accurately set and precisely maintained. For miters on stock less than 3" wide, set the miter fence at a 45° angle, and mill the workpiece standing on its edge. For miters on wider stock, set the tablesaw blade at 45°, return the miter fence to 90°, and lay the workpiece on its face. In either case, make trial cuts on scrap pieces first, to be sure settings are accurate.

5
Sanding

The most important element in the look of a box is the shine of its finished surfaces, and nothing can produce this except elbow grease, aided by the right sequence of abrasives. Sandpaper consists of a jumble of tiny rocks glued to a paper or cloth backing. These rocks engrave a pattern of grooves, like furrows plowed into a field, on the wood they are applied to. When a belt sander is used, these grooves are parallel and of uniform depth.

11

How deep is determined by the grit rating of the abrasive: as this number increases, groove depth decreases. A perfect finish is produced by repeated sanding with progressively finer grits, making these parallel grooves shallower until they become effectively invisible.

It is important to follow an orderly sequence of grits. Too broad a leap, such as going from coarse to very fine with nothing in between, doesn't work: trying to remove 60-grit scratches with a 220-grit abrasive will simply produce well-sanded scratches, for the 220x rocks are too small to obliterate the grooves the 60x rocks have made. When 60x is followed by 120x, then 180x, and finally a polishing belt, however, the result is a mirror-smooth surface.

Store-bought belts for the 6" x 48" sander are available up to about 180x, but even these leave scratches that will show as furry patches on the completed box. The solution is a polishing belt, created by making a well-worn 120x or 150x belt even less abrasive by further dulling its already rounded rocks. This can be done by carefully but re-
12

peatedly using the belt to sand a piece of heavy, resinous hardwood or soft metal, or by applying wax. A polishing belt is ready if no dust is visible coming off the end of the belt when it is in use. Although it takes some experimentation to produce, a good polishing belt can have the effect of 300x to 400x, and is ideal as the last in a series of progressively finer abrasive treatments.

Curved or irregular shapes cannot be polished on the flat platen of the belt sander, and the best means of bringing such surfaces to the desired mirror finish is hand or orbital sanding. Caution must be used with orbital sanders, however, as they occasionally leave circular scratches when crossing the grain, and can produce undesired round-overs as the pad passes over the edge of a workpiece. Hand sanding is always the best method, for unlike belts, sheet sandpaper is available in grits up to at least 600x. The more irregular the shape, and the harder the wood, the more time and effort will be needed to achieve a good finish.

Whatever tools are used, the sanding process

should be frequently interrupted to check the work with that best of all tools, the eye. A useful procedure for determining the exact condition of a surface is as follows. Hold the part in one hand and extend your arm straight. Pick a light source, such as a window or lightbulb, and aim your arm at it. Adjust the position of your hand until the alignment is just right, and the light will pick up every detail of the surface, and show even the tiniest scratches. When this extended-arm inspection no longer reveals any defects, the polishing process is complete, and the piece is ready for its liquid finish.

Other Sanding Operations

At some point, parts, assemblies, lids, and the like must be freed of the accumulated tool marks, glue, newspaper, clamp dents, tape adhesive, pencil notations, and other unwanted elements that mar exterior surfaces. In most instances, the belt sander is the tool of choice for this operation.

Selection of grit depends on the type of material to be removed. A coarse belt, such as 60x, is ideal for grinding off stubs of slip feathers and the dried glue around them. For a flat box part with only minor imperfections, in contrast, a sharp 150x belt is the best choice. It will not only remove the minimum amount necessary in the shortest time, but also prepare the surface for the next higher grit.

Many boxes have flat sides that meet at crisp mitered corners. When these corners are too crisp, their edges are so sharp they are uncomfortable to handle. More important, a too-sharp edge will inevitably collect tiny dings and dents, every one of which will be clearly visible. To prevent this, the sharp edges of a box should be lightly hand-sanded prior to final finish.

6
Assembly

The instructions for most of the boxes in this book call for inside surfaces to be sanded to finish-ready condition prior to assembly. Because it is usually impossible to do so afterwards, these parts are "polished" before glue-up, as described in Section 5. Before starting to glue up an assembly, it is always a good idea to go through a dry run, putting all the parts together first without the adhesive. This is particularly important with more complex assemblies. The dry run not only tests for fit, but also serves as a rehearsal of the assembly process, alerting the boxmaker to potential problems that may arise during time-sensitive glue-up. Another useful practice is testing every assembly for true, square, or plumb immediately after gluing, before it becomes too late to make necessary adjustments.

Adhesives

Aliphatic, or "white," glue, a convenient and economical adhesive, is appropriate for most projects. Epoxy or various types of waterproof glue may also be used. Glue should completely cover surfaces to be joined, and in general, too much glue is preferable to too little: a slight squeeze of excess is evidence that there is sufficient glue to hold the joint securely. Remember, however, that any excess will soon be rock hard, and difficult to remove without marring the carefully polished interior. To avoid this, let the glue dry until it reaches the consistency of stiff chewing gum (an hour or less). The excess may now be safely removed using a sharp chisel. To prevent unwanted bonding — such as gluing the box to the worktable, or the laminate strips to the clamping jig — use a single sheet of newspaper as a liner or separator. Despite its thinness, the newspaper will not be penetrated by the glue, and when dry, everything will sand neatly off.

Goop

No matter how carefully they are made, the joints in any project may show tiny gaps or voids, which must be filled prior to final sanding. Commercial wood fillers are available, but their colors are never quite right, especially when unusual woods are used. To prepare a custom-made filler or "goop," sand a scrap piece of the wood to be matched on the belt sander and carefully collect the resulting fine dust. Mix this with glue, and force the mixture into the gaps with the flat blade of an old chisel. Experiment to determine the proper consistency. If the proportion of glue to dust is too great, the result will be runny, and when dry will appear as a glue line; too little, the goop will be difficult to apply and will dry rough.

Clamping

Except for high pressure applications like gluing laminate strips, C-clamps are not widely used in boxmaking. For the small scale of most box assemblies, paper or cloth tape is usually the most effective clamp.

7
Finishing

Obtaining a beautiful finish has almost nothing to do with the product being used, and almost everything to do with the preparation of the surface to which it is applied. The deep, silken liquid look of a perfect finish, with the feeling of being able to see right down into the wood, comes not from obscure ingredients or arcane compounds, but from time and the elbow grease so frequently referred to in this introduction. Once the right

wood has been selected, all that is required to bring out its natural beauty is the proper surface preparation. The depressing custom of drowning fine woods such as mahogany, walnut, oak, or cherry in a brown or reddish stain may be justifiable where poorly matched or inappropriate woods must be used, but it has no place in fine boxmaking.

Varnish and Lacquer Versus Penetrating Oil

Two general types of clear finish are used in the projects in this book: penetrating oil, which soaks into the wood and then hardens, and varnish or lacquer, which lies on top of it. Varnish is the finish of choice in projects where contact with liquids is likely. Polyurethane is the most common type, and should be applied following manufacturer's instructions in at least three coats. Lacquer's quick drying time makes it easier to work with than varnish, but lacquer is not as durable nor as water-resistant. Furthermore, its thinner nature means that more coats are needed to produce a satisfactory finish.

Penetrating oil finishes show off dramatic figure and grain patterns better than lacquer or varnish, whose multiple coats covering the surface tend to fill the pores of the wood. Oil finishes are relatively simple to apply, and have the advantage of not requiring a dust-free environment. Oil can be applied with a cloth, and rubbed in with fine steel wool. When the surface is dry, steel wool is again used to smooth it. The final step is to apply an appropriate wax, which can be buffed to high lustre by hand or with a buffing wheel.

8
Final Touches

Among the many pleasures of the box, one of the greatest is the sense of anticipation as it is opened. Remember that the mystery of the interior is part of the essence, so make the inside as nice as the outside whenever possible. Lining the bottom with a lush material such as velvet or suede adds to the visual excitement, and also provides a practical way to protect both the box and its treasured contents.

Many of the boxes in this book are lined. For lining interiors, drawers, and compartments, one technique is to glue the lining material directly to the wood. A more elegant approach is to wrap the material around a piece of mat board, available from art-supply and picture-frame stores, to produce a tight-fitting pad. For small or irregularly shaped areas, flocking is a good solution.

Finally, use an electric engraver or other tool to sign, number, and/or date the box, and to list the woods used, or add an inscription or dedication.

9
Safety

Woodworking is inherently dangerous. The raw material itself can be heavy, sharp-edged, and splintery, and the tools used to fabricate it are all potentially lethal. These factors, combined with noxious dust, harmful chemicals, high noise levels, and large quantities of electricity, produce an environment in which disfiguring, crippling, or even fatal injury can occur in dozens of unforeseen ways. To operate a safe woodshop, always keep this in mind.

The risk of injury can never be completely removed, but it can be reduced to an acceptable level by strict observation of certain guidelines.

1

For safe operation of all tools, fully understand and adhere to the manufacturer's instructions.

2

Never allow fingers to come near any moving blade or cutter. Use a push stick.

3

Always wear a respirator or dust mask in the shop. Always wear ear and eye protection when using power tools.

4

Always wear appropriate clothing. A heavy work apron will protect the midsection from the occasional table-saw kickback. A dropped chisel hurts less on a protected toe than on a bare one; do not wear sandals in the shop.

5

Never perform any operation without being satisfied that you understand it and are comfortable with it.

6

Keep your mind on the work. Do not allow your attention to wander, especially when performing any repetitive operations.

7

Never work when tired, in a hurry, or simply not in the mood to work. It is better to stop, or find something to do outside the shop for a while. Return refreshed and in the proper frame of mind.

KNITTING BOX

By Graham Blackburn

Graham Blackburn is a writer, an illustrator, and a custom furniture maker. He has been the editor of Woodwork *and a contributing editor to* Fine Woodworking *and* Popular Woodworking *and writes regularly for various magazines in the crafts field.*

Blackburn has published 15 books and was featured in Maxine Rosenberg's Artists of Handcrafted Furniture at Work *and Jane Smiley's* Catskill Crafts: Artisans of the Catskill Mountains.

Besides furniture making, teaching, and his writing and illustrating commitments, Blackburn has made numerous television appearances as a home-repair consultant.

About This Box:

A proper knitting box is basic equipment for anyone who knits for a living, and Graham Blackburn designed this example to the exacting specifications of a professional.

The sleek simplicity of this box is heightened by ebony feet, which raise it slightly, and a solid ebony panel in the lid. This panel is milled with a thin keel all around, which fits into a slot in the purpleheart frame, to allow for expansion and contraction of the solid wood. The lid and body of the box are glued up together, as a single unit, and the lid is later sliced off. Vertical splines reinforce the miter joints. The dividers on which the trays rest are removable, allowing the storage configuration to be changed. Blackburn has reinforced the tray joints with tiny brass pins, and glued on the wood tray bottoms so that their edges are visible.

Part	Description	Dimensions	Qty.
A	Lid panel	11-1/4 x 9 x 1/2	1
B	Lid frame	8-1/2 x 3-1/4 x 1/2	1
C	Lid frame	17-3/8 x 1-3/4 x 1/2	2
D	Lid side	17-3/8 x 3/4 x 9/16	2
E	Lid side	11-7/8 x 3/4 x 9/16	2
F	Handle	3-1/2 x 7/8 x 1/2	1
G	Side	17-3/8 x 3-1/2 x 9/16	2
H	Side	11-7/8 x 3-1/2 x 9/16	2
J	Divider	10-7/8 x 2-3/4 x 1/2	2
K	Mitered tray rest	10-7/8 x 1-3/4 x 1/4	4
L	Mitered tray rest	8 x 1-3/4 x 1/4	4
M	Bottom	16-3/4 x 11-1/2 x 1/4	1
N	Spline	3-1/2 x 1/2 x 1/8	4
O	Foot	17 x 1 x 1/2	2
P	Foot	11-1/2 x 1 x 1/2	2
Q	Tray side	5-5/16 x 1-3/4 x 5/16	2
R	Tray side	7-7/8 x 1-3/4 x 5/16	2
S	Tray bottom	7-7/8 x 5-5/16 x 1/8	1
T	Brass hinge	1-1/2 x 1	2

See Diagram on page 19.

KNITTING BOX DIAGRAM

By Graham Blackburn

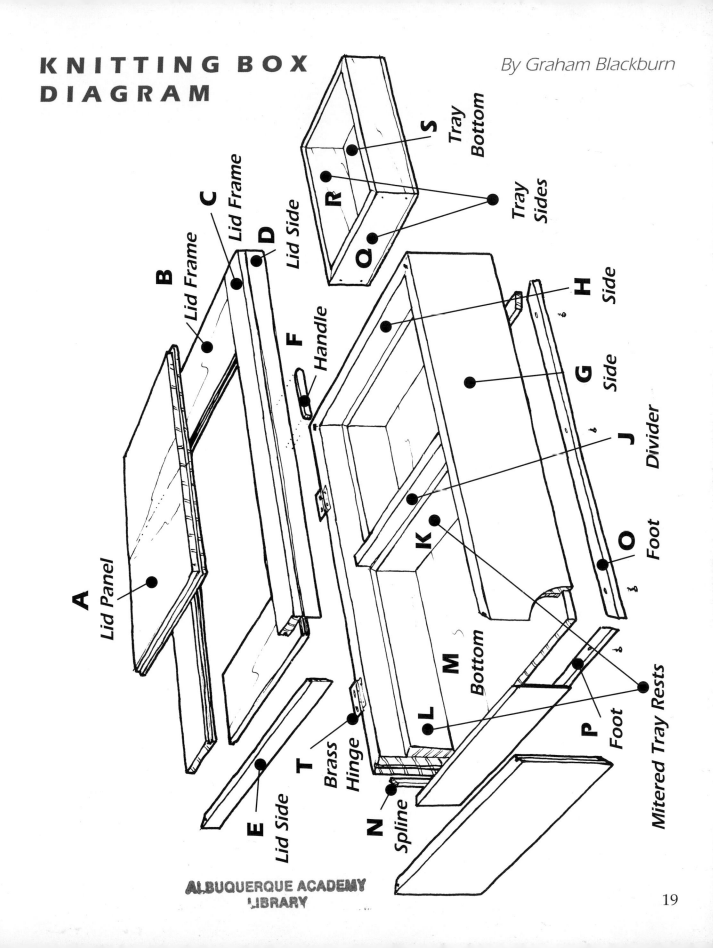

A — Lid Panel
B — Lid Frame
C — Lid Frame
D — Lid Side
E — Lid Side
F — Handle
G — Side
H — Side
J — Divider
K —
L — Bottom
M — Bottom
N — Spline
O — Foot
P — Foot
Q — Tray Sides
R —
S — Tray Bottom
T — Brass Hinge
— Mitered Tray Rests
— Tray Sides

DRIFTWOOD TAMBOUR BOX

By Ted Box

Raised on Long Island, Ted Box began his woodworking career at age fourteen when he built his first boat. "I loved the craft of boat building, but there just wasn't enough room for creativity. One day, I was walking along the beach and tripped over a piece of driftwood. Picking it up, I saw a desk in it, and that got me headed to where I am now."

Ted Box uses driftwood for furniture as well as for boxes. This rustic, rough-hewn material — with a decidedly outdoor feeling to it — is entirely unexpected in a home environment such as a living room, dining room or kitchen.

"The other day, my fourteen-year-old son came up with the best description I've heard for what I do. Looking at one of my new pieces, he said, 'Dad, that looks like something a wizard would own.'"

About This Box:

No boxmaker can come home from walking an ocean beach without a head filled with dreams of boxes made of driftwood.

This sleek gray flotsam, with its fabulous salt-weathered patina and dramatic random shapes, begs to be turned into beautiful objects. Driftwood, unfortunately, can be brittle, sand-encrusted, and/or water-logged, and only the most determined woodworker can find ways to use it.

Ted Box has the necessary determination, and because he lives on Martha's Vineyard, driving for a few miles in any direction brings him to the lumberyard. In this tambour, or roll-top, box, Box gives new life to woods collected from Vineyard beaches.

Part	Description	Dimensions	Qty.
A	Tambour	10-1/2 x 9-1/2 x 1/2	20
B	Top	12-3/4 x 8-1/2 x 1	1
C	Side	11-1/4 x 10-1/2 x 1	2
D	Back	10 x 9-1/2 x 1	1
E	Shelf back	10 x 5 x 3/4	1
F	Top shelf	10 x 2 x 1/4	1
G	Shelf support	2 x 1-1/2 x 1/2	2
H	Bottom shelf	8-1/2 x 2 x 1/4	1
J	Bottom	10 x 8 x 1	1
K	Front apron	8 x 1-1/2 x 1/2	1
L	Vine trim	1/2 diameter x 8	1

See Diagram on page 23.

DRIFTWOOD TAMBOUR BOX DIAGRAM

By Ted Box

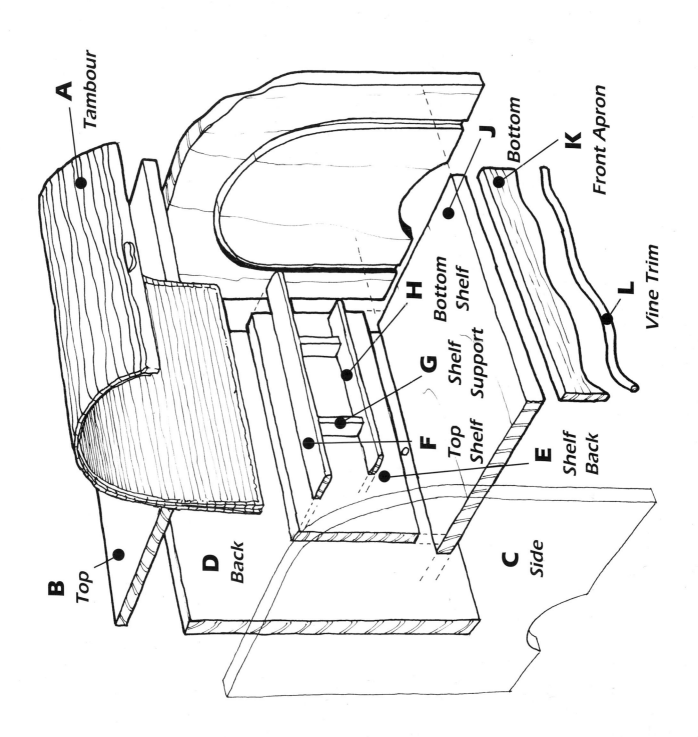

A — Tambour
B — Top
C — Side
D — Back
E — Shelf Back
F — Top Shelf
G — Shelf Support
H — Bottom Shelf
J — Bottom
K — Front Apron
L — Vine Trim

YIN-YANG BOX

By Craig Brown

Craig Brown is a self-taught woodworker residing in beautiful northern Michigan. His career began in 1981 when a lifelong interest in woodworking evolved into an intense study and development of his skills. After overwhelming encouragement, he began the transition to full-time designer-craftsman.

Brown's work has gone in many directions. He was first involved in commercial/residential architectural woodwork and custom furniture. Since 1986, he has concentrated on designing and crafting beautiful small wooden boxes — which is the heart of his work.

His boxes are sold at some 70 galleries internationally. Brown also exhibits at several art fairs yearly, including the highly acclaimed Ann Arbor Art Fair.

His unique jewelry boxes, and more recently the fine fly boxes he's designed, are the result of his continuing growth and a desire to create something beautiful and useful with his own hands. To design and craft a piece of woodwork and to see a rough board transformed into a functional object is a great reward.

About This Box:

The moment of opening is among the most fascinating things about a box, and Craig Brown has dramatized the moment in this deceptively simple-looking design.

He separated the lid into two halves, and gave one a concave and the other a convex profile. This same-but-different motif is repeated in the contrasting woods, wenge and maple, and the lid evokes the ancient, mystical union of opposites.

The box is constructed using finger joints, and the sides are shaped and sanded to produce their satisfying curves. The pins on which the two lid halves pivot are located squarely in the middle of each side. Because of the way they are shaped, however, these halves move in a subtly off-center manner: opening and closing this box is endlessly fascinating.

Part	Description	Dimensions	Qty.
A	Top	5 x 2-1/2 x 3/4	2
B	Side	5 x 3/4 x 1-1/8	2
C	Side	5 x 3/4 x 1-1/8	2
D	Bottom	3-1/2 x 3-1/2 x 1/4	1
E	Lid pivot pin	1/8 x 1	2

See Diagram on page 27.

YIN-YANG BOX DIAGRAM

By Craig Brown

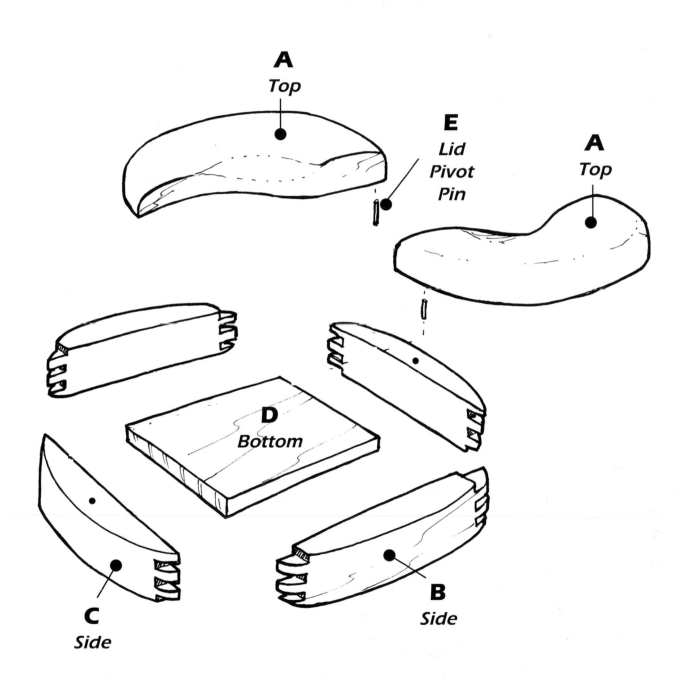

A
Top

E
Lid Pivot Pin

A
Top

D
Bottom

C
Side

B
Side

DRY-FLY BOX

By Craig Brown

About This Box:

Not many boxmakers are confident enough of their technical abilities to produce a box that is deliberately designed to be taken on a fishing trip, but that is just what Craig Brown has done with his box for storing dry flies. As with his preceding design, Brown utilizes finger joints, whose great strength is well suited to the kind of real-world use a fly box is likely to get. The hinge pins that hold the two halves of the box together are spring-loaded. The sharp points of the fishhooks are set in cork strips, each backed by a profiled wood stiffener, which are glued to the inside of the box. The two halves are kept shut by an ingenious spring-loaded catch Brown has built, whose tongue fastens in a tiny slot. The box shown is made of lacewood, and Brown also produces this box in maple and other strong hardwoods.

Part	Description	Dimensions	Qty.
A	Top	5-1/2 x 3-1/2 x 1/8	2
B	Side	4 x 3/4 x 1/4	4
C	Hinge side	5-1/2 x 3/4 x 1/4	1
D	Hinge side	5-1/2 x 3/4 x 1/4	1
E	Strike side	5-1/2 x 3/4 x 1/4	1
F	Latch side	5-1/2 x 3/4 x 1/4	1
G	Latch	5/8 x 1/2 x 1/4	1
H	Hinge pin, spring loaded	1/16 x 1/2	3
J	Fly rack	3-1/2 x 1/8 x 1/8	12

See Diagram on page 30.

DRY-FLY BOX DIAGRAM

By Craig Brown

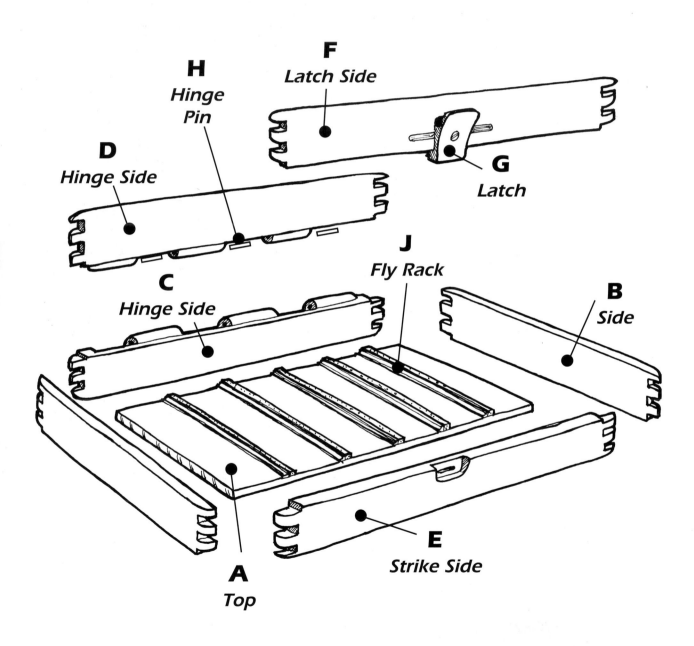

F
Latch Side

H
Hinge Pin

D
Hinge Side

G
Latch

C
Hinge Side

J
Fly Rack

B
Side

E
Strike Side

A
Top

TEMPLE BOX
DIAGRAM: 1 of 2

By Marc Coan

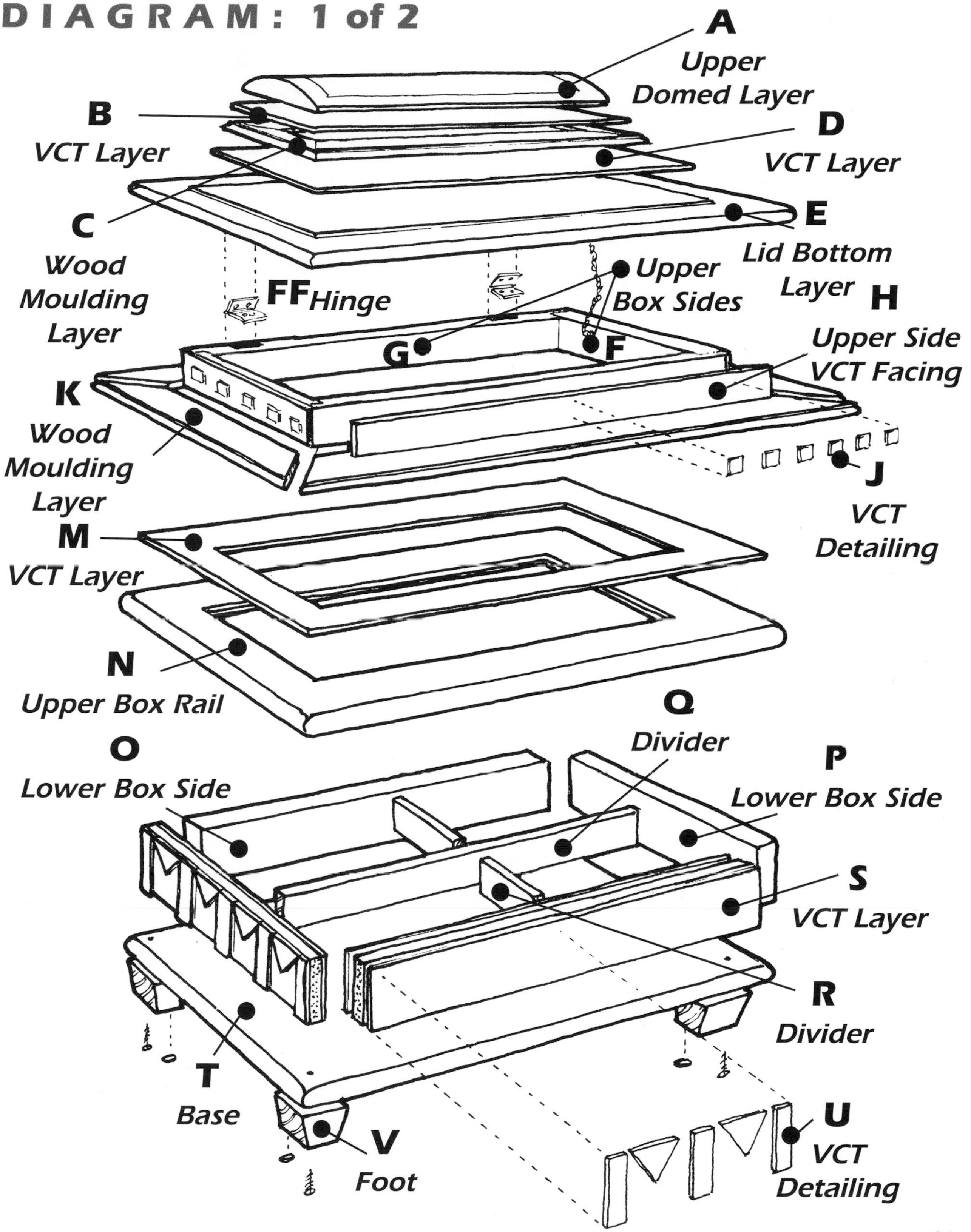

A Upper Domed Layer

B VCT Layer

D VCT Layer

C Wood Moulding Layer

E Lid Bottom Layer

FF Hinge

Upper Box Sides

G

F

H Upper Side VCT Facing

K Wood Moulding Layer

J VCT Detailing

M VCT Layer

N Upper Box Rail

Q Divider

O Lower Box Side

P Lower Box Side

S VCT Layer

R Divider

T Base

V Foot

U VCT Detailing

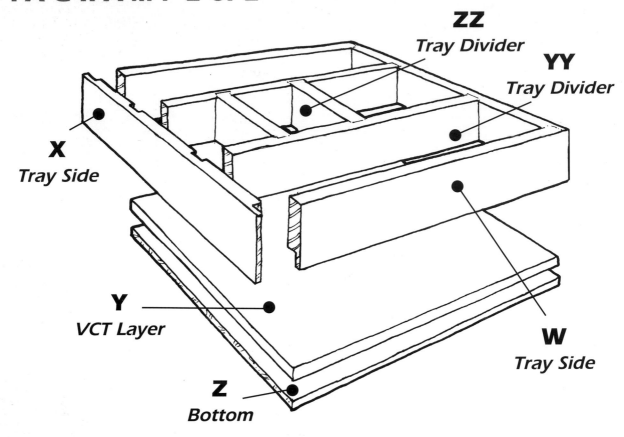

ZZ *Tray Divider*

YY *Tray Divider*

X *Tray Side*

Y *VCT Layer*

Z *Bottom*

W *Tray Side*

Continued from page 35.

Part	Description	Dimensions	Qty.
P	Lower box side	9 x 1-3/4 x 1/2	2
Q	Divider	13 x 1-1/4 x 1/4	1
R	Divider	3-1/2 x 1-1/4 x 1/4	2
S	VCT layer	14-1/4 x 1-3/4 x 1/8	2
T	Base	16 x 10 x 1/2	1
U	VCT detailing	As required	*
V	Foot	1-1/8 x 1-1/8 x 1-1/8	4
W	Tray side	6-1/2 x 1-1/4 x 1/4	2
X	Tray side	6-3/4 x 1-1/4 x 1/4	2
Y	VCT layer	6-1/2 x 6-1/2 x 1/8	1
Z	Bottom	6-1/2 x 6-1/2 x 1/8	1
YY	Tray divider	6-1/2 x 1 x 1/4	2
ZZ	Tray divider	2-1/8 x 1 x 1/4	2

* As required

TEMPLE BOX

By Marc Coan

Marc Coan grew up in the Southwest, and like many box-makers, his designs have been influenced by the architecture of his native region. Among his first influences were the Spanish- and Pueblo-style buildings of New Mexico, whose fusion of classical proportions with climate-appropriate native materials make them both habitable and long-lasting.

While travelling, Coan takes pictures of any buildings that interest him or that he finds unusual, later using these as a reference library of design possibilities.

Most recently, Coan has been experimenting with a material called vinyl composition tile (VCT). It is used for flooring, but the colors and patterns are so vivid that Coan loves using it for his own unorthodox purposes. "I'm always searching for ways to fuse the beauty of natural woods with faux finishes and mixed-media accents, like the colorful vinyl tiles," he says. "These new boxes are a natural outgrowth of all the work I've created up to now."

About This Box:

For years, Marc Coan has been experimenting with ways of combining fine hardwood with unusual textures, colors, and finishes. His studio in New Mexico, typically filled with ongoing airbrushed furniture, mirror, and picture frame projects, has recently been invaded by two of his newest fascinations: vinyl composition tile and copper paint with a chemical patina.

This Temple Box, with its commanding architectural presence and satisfying, timeless proportions, is the fruit of his recent explorations. The box is constructed of a series of layers of hardwood, painted wood, and tile, with small pieces of tile for additional surface decoration. The hinged lid opens to reveal a tray, which Coan has divided into sections, atop a larger compartment, also divided.

Part	Description	Dimensions	Qty.
A	Upper domed layer	12-1/2 x 6-1/2 x 3/4	1
B	VCT layer	13 x 7 x 1/8	1
C	Wood moulding layer	7-1/2 x 3-1/2 x 3/8	1
D	VCT layer	14 x 8 x 1/8	1
E	Lid bottom layer	15 x 9 x 1/2	1
F	Upper box side	7-1/4 x 1-1/4 x 5/8	2
FF	Hinge	1-1/2 x 1	2
G	Upper box side	14 x 1-1/4 x 5/8	2
H	Upper side VCT facing	As required	*
J	VCT detailing	As required	*
K	Wood moulding layer	15-1/2 x 9 x 3/8	1
M	VCT layer	15-3/4 x 9-3/4 x 1/8	1
N	Upper box rail	16 x 10 x 1/2	1
O	Lower box side	14 x 1-3/4 x 1/2	2

Continued on page 32.

See Diagrams on pages 31 and 32.

*As required

SILVER CHEST

By Charles Cobb

Charles Cobb is a self-taught woodworker who holds a Bachelor of Fine Arts degree from the Art Center College of Design at Pasadena, California.

Cobb mills his own lumber, preferring to leave the natural edge on his boards. The drawer on his featured silverware chest came to him as a piece of firewood. He experiments with a variety of woods and shapes to create his pieces, rarely repeating a design. Specializing in unique containers, Cobb also builds tables, desks, handrails, and mantels.

Cobb has juried more than 30 shows and fairs and his work has been exhibited in the U.C. Berkeley Museum at Blackhawk in Danville, California, the Nevada Museum of Art in Reno, the Bakersfield Art Museum in California, as well as galleries in several states. He has been featured in many publications.

About This Box:

The dramatic architectural form of this stunning silver chest is characteristic of the work of California designer Charles Cobb. The body of the chest is made from a single 14"-wide slab of 1"-thick narra.

The drawer fronts are a book-matched piece of solid walnut; the black wood used to accent the legs and handle, and to make the rounded feet, is wenge.

Cobb has used a five-layer solid-wood laminate for the handle and flying buttress legs of this piece. The central section of each leg is 1/2"-thick narra, flanked on either side by 1/4"-thick pieces of wenge and figured walnut. (The wenge, being in the middle, appears only as a band.) The handle also follows this five-layer pattern.

The upper drawer slides out to reveal a custom-made rack for sterling flatware, while a similar rack in the wedge-shaped lower drawer stores the larger serving utensils.

Cobb has decorated his design with an intricate but barely visible pattern of dots, produced by 1/8" dowel plugs, milled from wood slightly lighter than the narra or walnut into which they are inserted. These dots border the top, sides, and legs of his piece, some running along the edge, others clustered in symmetrical groupings of three, four, or five.

LEGGED BOX

By Tom Davin and Mary Kessler

Tom Davin and Mary Kessler met in a college art class. Mary remembers, "Tom was always working in the woodshop, so if I wanted to see him that's where I'd go. I'm not the kind of person who could sit there and do nothing, so I began to help out. One thing led to another, and it wasn't long before our woodwork was helping to put both of us through college."

Tom and Mary's success comes from their ability to combine creative design, skillful production, and good business sense. A visit to their booth at a crafts fair reveals an eye-catching assortment of highly functional objects, from letter openers to boxes to chopsticks, each with the bold but graceful shapes that have become their trademark.

"Tom is the main designer and the powerhouse in the shop," Mary notes at their Rhode Island studio. "He's particularly good at making the jigs and templates we need to produce multiples. Now that we have three kids, I've been spending less time in the shop and more time making sure we're running things in a businesslike way."

About This Box:

Tom Davin and Mary Kessler developed this intriguing design by starting with a straightforward rectangular box, and making three simple but important transformations. They angled the front and back (raising the lower edges in a slight curve), added a visually striking handle, and supported the whole on four gracefully curved legs. The resulting design preserves the satisfying four-square feeling of the basic box, but makes it more interesting and distinctive.

The legs and body of the box are walnut. Tom and Mary have carefully selected for the front a piece of walnut with a ripple of curl, while using darker, straight-grained wood for the legs. The lid and the two lift ornaments are rosewood; the lift is walnut.

Maple Treasury on page 44 is another example of their unique style.

Part	Description	Dimensions	Qty.
A	Top	9 x 4-1/4 x 1/4	1
B	Side	9-3/4 x 2-5/8 x 3/8	2
C	Side	5-1/4 x 2-5/8 x 3/8	2
D	Bottom	9-1/4 x 5-1/2 x 1/8	1
E	Lift	3-3/4 x 3/4 x 1/4	1
F	Lift ornament	1-3/4 x 1/4 x 1/4	2
G	Leg	3-1/4 x 7/8 x 7/8	4
H	Hinge pin	3/8 x 1/16	2

See Diagram on page 40.

LEGGED BOX DIAGRAM

By Tom Davin and Mary Kessler

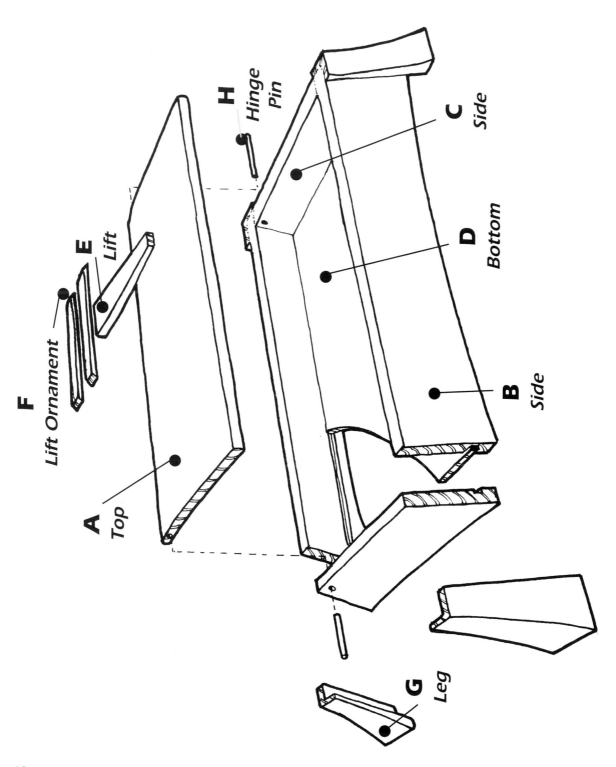

F
Lift Ornament

E
Lift

A
Top

H
Hinge Pin

C
Side

D
Bottom

B
Side

G
Leg

OVAL BOX DIAGRAM

By Tom Davin and Mary Kessler

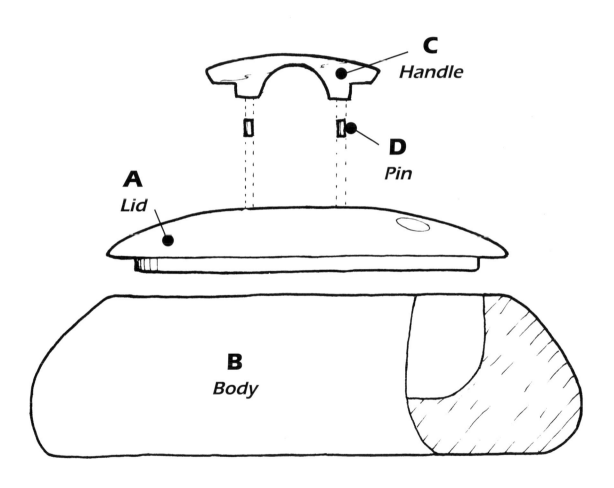

C
Handle

D
Pin

A
Lid

B
Body

OVAL BOX

By Tom Davin and Mary Kessler

About This Box:

The word "box" tends to suggest right angles, squares, and rectangles, but in this project, Tom Davin and Mary Kessler show the marvellous results that can come from a day spent avoiding straight lines.

The body of this box is shaped from a single block of wood. If there's a thick but short chunk of interesting wood lying around your workshop, this is the ideal project for it. (Tom and Mary's chunk was walnut, with rosewood for the lid.) While it's still a rectangle, rout out the interior, then rough shape into an oval on the belt sander using a coarse (40x to 60x) belt. Continue this process using successively finer belts until the shape is perfected, concluding by fine sanding using a vibrating sander.

Make the lid using contrasting wood, and add a handle as shown, or provide your own variation.

Part	Description	Dimensions	Qty.
A	Lid	5 x 3 x 3/4	1
B	Body	6-1/2 x 4 x 1-3/4	1
C	Handle	2-1/2 x 5/8 x 3/8	1
D	Pin	1/16 x 1/2	2

See Diagram on page 41.

MAPLE TREASURY

By Tom Davin and Mary Kessler

About This Box:

Boxmakers are often asked to create a box with two distinct features: the storage capacity of drawers, and the ready access of a hinged lid. In response to this design challenge, Davin and Kessler produced Maple Treasury, a simple and clean-lined solution done in bird's-eye maple with rosewood detailing.

The approach they've taken is to expand on their Legged Box, shown on page 38. Because of its larger size and scale, the drawer box needs a more architectural feel, and this has led to several modifications. First, the delicate curves of the smaller legged box mature into Maple Treasury's sturdy angled corners, evoking strength, repose, and timelessness. A second storey appears, the corners of its overhanging eaves accented by rosewood slip feathers, echoing the rosewood of the drawer handles. Finally, to suggest the dome of the building's roof, the lid is bevelled.

DOVETAIL BOX

By Michael Elkan

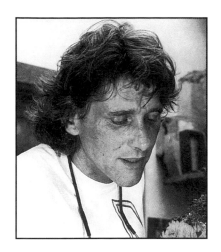

Michael Elkan was raised in Philadelphia and became a successful knitwear designer. His knitwear creations were featured in many magazines, such as Esquire *and* Playboy.

After years of the fast and furious pace in this line of work, Elkan felt a calling to the gentle quiet of the West Coast, and relocated to Oregon. He worked again in the clothing industry as a designer and travelled extensively, but he loved being home enjoying walks through the forests with his wife, Sharon, as he had grown up in a neighborhood where not a single tree grew.

It was on one of those walks that they came across a fascinating piece of burl. He carried it home and decided to see what he could "turn it into." The rest is history and today his works, from small wooden boxes to elaborate custom furniture, are found in private collections everywhere.

The main focus in his woodworking is taking a single piece of wood — "a chunk of nature" — and, using its own natural beauty, turning it into a masterpiece.

About This Box:

Although Michael Elkan is primarily known for his sculptural work in burl (see photos on pages 52 and 53), he also enjoys a national reputation for his functional pieces. In this design, Elkan has simplified the concept of the box to its fundamental elements: a body and a lid. Dispensing with complications like separate sides, bottoms, miters, joinery, hinges, glue, or splines, this box consists of just two pieces of wood, accompanied by one piece of metal and a screw.

The body of the box is routed out, and the mating dovetail slots in the lid and body are routed with a dovetail bit. To provide a snug fit for the lid without the risk of the wood swelling and seizing up, Elkan has added Part C, a simple metal pressure spring.

Part	Description	Dimensions	Qty.
A	Lid	7 x 4 x 5/8	1
B	Body	7 x 4 x 7/8	1
C	Pressure spring	1/8 x 1-1/8	1

See Diagram on page 48.

DOVETAIL BOX
DIAGRAM

By Michael Elkan

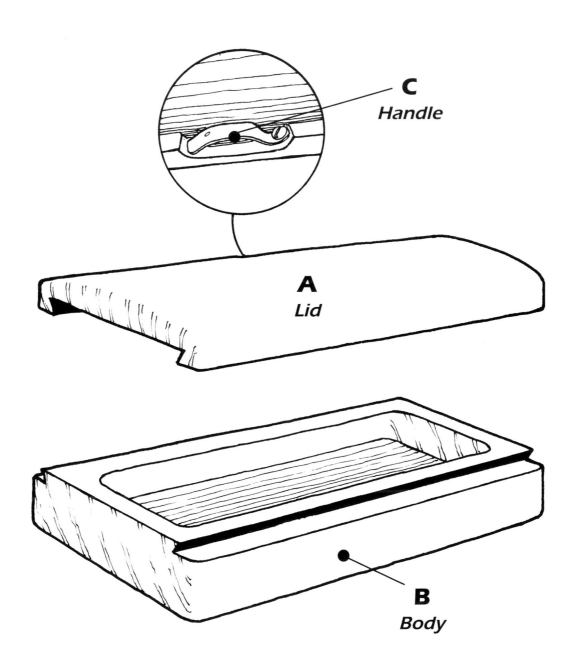

C
Handle

A
Lid

B
Body

DRAWER BOX DIAGRAM

By Michael Elkan

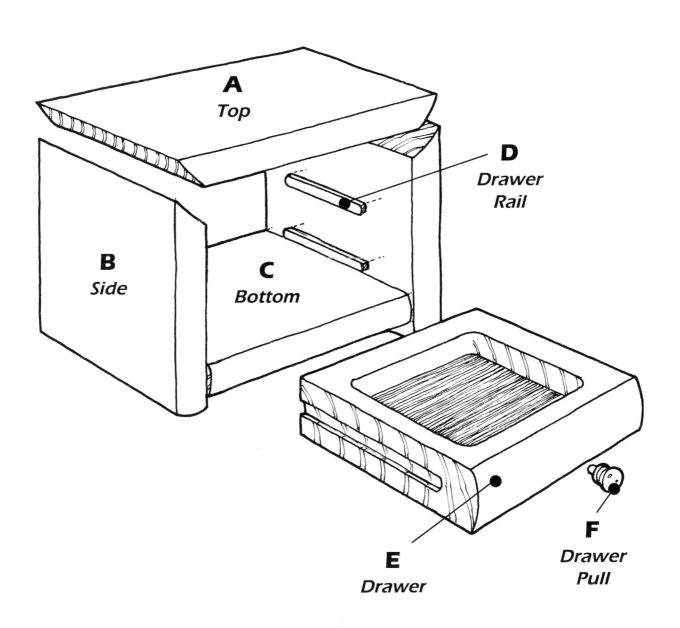

A
Top

D
Drawer Rail

B
Side

C
Bottom

E
Drawer

F
Drawer Pull

DRAWER BOX

By Michael Elkan

About This Box:

This easy-to-make box looks great in a variety of wood combinations, and is easily adapted for any number of drawers. (Versions with two drawers and six drawers appear in the accompanying drawing and photographs.) Drawers are made from a single piece of wood, with the interior space routed, so there is a minimum of construction.

Each drawer has two slots routed on its sides, and the drawers slide on rails glued to the inside walls of the body. The woods shown are walnut and western maple.

Part	Description	Dimensions	Qty.
A	Top	6-1/2 x 5 x 3/4	1
B	Side	4-3/4 x 5 x 3/4	2
C	Bottom	4-7/8 x 5 x 3/4	1
D	Drawer rail	3-1/2 x 1/4 x 1/4	4
E	Drawer	5 x 4-7/8 x 1-3/8	2
F	Drawer pull	1/2 x 3/4	2

See Diagram on page 49.

NO-WAY STAIRWAY

By Michael Elkan

About This Box:

Trees occasionally produce irregular growth patterns, such as bird's-eyes or burls, in much the same way an oyster creates a pearl to insulate itself from an irritating grain of sand. These irregularities make the lumber unsuitable for ordinary uses, such as construction, flooring, or cabinetry, but ideal for boxmakers like Michael Elkan. From his studio in the Oregon woods, Elkan places western maple burl in startling new contexts, emphasizing its sculptural quality while celebrating the organic beauty of its natural form. No-Way Stairway is the title of this piece, carved from a single burl, which includes in its complex shape four lidded boxes.

HANDYMAN'S TEA BOX

By Glenn Elvig

Glenn Elvig's career as a craftsperson began in high school when he and a ceramics teacher bought a kiln to produce functional stoneware. "I'd wanted to be an artist since I was four years old," Elvig recalls, "and I started out selling my pots in eleventh grade."

Receiving a degree in Art Education, Elvig taught for several years, but soon realized that teaching art was no substitute for making art. Elvig then resolved to start his own studio in Minneapolis.

He first exhibited his sculptural boxes and wall hangings at the American Craft Council's 1987 Winter Market in Baltimore, Maryland, where his designs sold well. Three years later, at the ACC's Armory Show in New York, the response to his work was overwhelming.

Although demand for Elvig's work is increasing as he is discovered by collectors worldwide, the artist maintains his own goal: "I just want to continue creating the work I want to create. If I can keep on doing that, I feel I'm more than rich."

About This Box:

Glenn Elvig has created a series of tea boxes, one for each letter of the alphabet, entitled *Twenty-Six Tease*. In this one, which Elvig calls Handyman's Tea, he has attached tools, hardware, and other familiar household objects to a maple frame. When opened, the box reveals its function as a tea caddy, with plenty of room for the tea it was designed to hold.

STEP-TANSU

By John Reed Fox

John Reed Fox is drawn to woodworking through his love for crafting one-of-a-kind objects. In harmony with the nature of the art, he prefers traditional Japanese hand tools, including saws and planes manufactured in Japan.

A self-taught woodworker, he has been designing and building unique furniture since 1979. He says that Japanese housewares and architecture are major influences. A graceful merging of the functional with the decorative is reflected in Fox's works, which are clean and elegant. He treats joinery as both a structural and a decorative element.

The relationship between craftsperson, materials, tools, and methods is the most essential element in his work. He prefers domestic woods, such as cherry and walnut, for their subtlety.

Fox's work has been published in The New York Times, *American Craft Magazine, and* Woodwork Magazine, *and has appeared in art shows in Washington, D.C., Pennsylvania, and Massachusetts, where he resides.*

About This Box:

The intriguing shape of this box with drawers, based on the traditional Japanese Step-Tansu, is typical of the work of John Reed Fox, whose designs preserve the integrity of classical forms, while reflecting his own distinctive touch.

This Tansu box is simple to make, and lends itself to endless variation. The lucky person who gets to own the finished product will find it as much a sculpture as a place for storage, and the horizontal surfaces are ideal platforms for interesting small objects. Fox deliberately uses woods with quiet color and grain pattern—this box is cherry—but it is easy to imagine this piece in any number of woods. The joints are held together with splines, and the traditional pulls are wrought iron.

Part	Description	Dimensions	Qty.
A	Plate	8-1/4 x 6-7/8 x 1/2	2
B	Side	9-1/8 x 8-1/4 x 1/2	1
C	Riser	8-1/4 x 2-1/8 x 1/2	3
D	Plate	10-1/2 x 8-1/4 x 1/2	1
E	Plate	14 x 8-1/4 x 1/2	1
F	Riser	8-1/4 x 2-3/4 x 1/2	1
G	Bottom	17-1/2 x 8-1/4 x 1/2	1
H	Drawer stop	1 x 1/2 x 1/16	5
J	Spline	7-3/4 x 1/2 x 1/8	12
K	Drawer bay back	As required	5
L	Drawer front / back (varies)	8 x 2-3/8 x 3/4	2
M	Drawer top/bottom	6-5/8 x 2-3/8 x 1/2	2
N	Drawer shelf	As required	2
O	Drawer front / back (varies)	6-5/8 x 1-1/2 x 3/4	2
P	Drawer side	6-5/8 x 1-1/2 x 1/2	2
Q	Drawer bottom	6 x 6 x 1/4	1
R	Iron pull		5

See Diagrams on page 58.

STEP-TANSU DIAGRAMS

By John Reed Fox

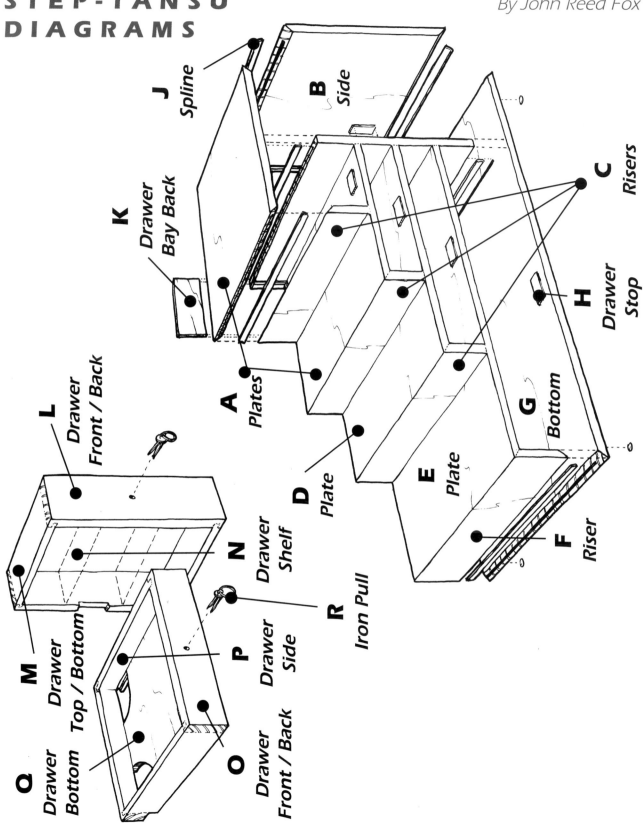

J *Spline*

B *Side*

C *Risers*

K *Drawer Bay Back*

H *Drawer Stop*

A *Plates*

L *Drawer Front / Back*

G *Bottom*

D *Plate*

E *Plate*

F *Riser*

N *Drawer Shelf*

R *Iron Pull*

M *Drawer Top / Bottom*

P *Drawer Side*

Q *Drawer Bottom*

O *Drawer Front / Back*

JASMINE JEWELRY BOX DIAGRAM

By John Reed Fox

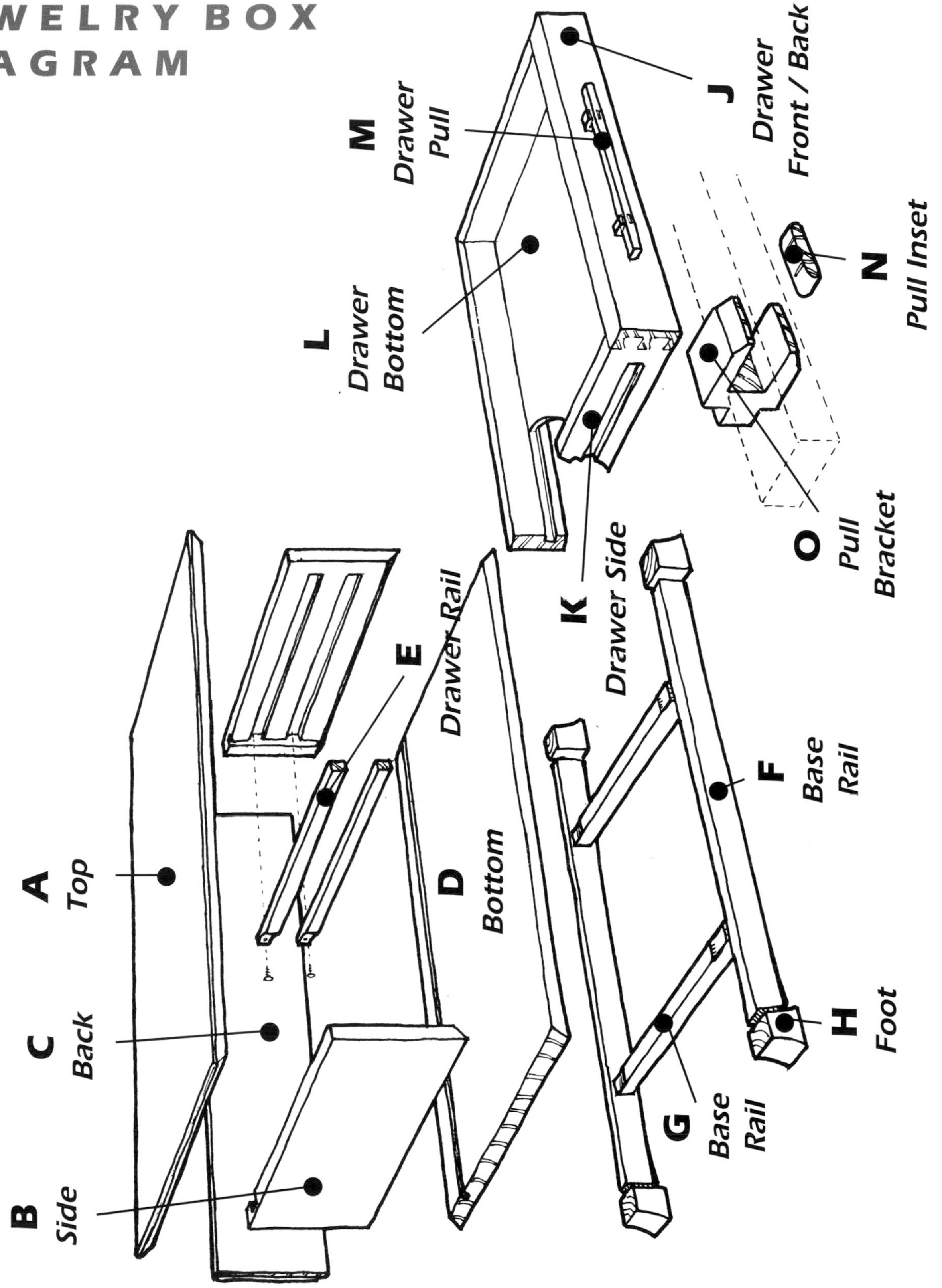

A Top

B Side

C Back

D Bottom

E Drawer Rail

F Base Rail

G Base Rail

H Foot

J Drawer Front / Back

K Drawer Side

L Drawer Bottom

M Drawer Pull

N Pull Inset

O Pull Bracket

JASMINE JEWELRY BOX

By John Reed Fox

About This Box:

The design of this rosewood and satinwood jewelry box by John Reed Fox seems to suggest ancient origins, yet it is distinctively contemporary.

Construction of the body, lid, and drawers is straightforward, but the drawer handles and the detailing of the base reflect some of the subtle complexities that mark the Fox style.

The solid drawer pulls are mounted in brackets ornamented with inlaid plugs. The front and back rails of the base are slightly lower than the cross rails, allowing a slight but crucial reveal between the bottom of the box and the top of the base.

Part	Description	Dimensions	Qty.
A	Top	15-3/4 x 10-3/8 x 3/4	1
B	Side	9 x 4-1/4 x 3/4	2
C	Back	13 x 4-1/8 x 1/2	1
D	Bottom	13-1/2 x 9 x 3/4	1
E	Drawer rail	7-1/4 x 3/8 x 1/2	4
F	Base rail	12-1/4 x 3/4 x 9/16	2
G	Base rail	8 x 3/4 x 9/16	2
H	Foot	1-1/8 x 7/8 x 7/8	4
J	Drawer front / back	12-1/2 x 1-3/4 x 1/2	4
K	Drawer side	8-3/8 x 1-3/4 x 1/2	4
L	Drawer bottom	12 x 7-3/4 x 1/8	2
M	Drawer pull	5-1/2 x 5/8 x 3/8	2
N	Pull inset	7/16 x 1/8 x 1/8	4
O	Pull bracket	5/8 x 7/8 x 3/4	4

See Diagram on page 59.

CONTEMPORARY SILVER CHEST

By Michael Killigrew

Michael Killigrew studied fine furniture making at the College of the Redwoods with cabinetmaker James Krenov. Killigrew's work has been shown at numerous exhibitions throughout California, and most recently, his Silver Chest was featured at the Celebration of Sierra Woods exhibition in Nevada City.

Since age 12, Killigrew's interest in woodworking has been nurtured under the guidance of Robert Erickson, the country's leading chairmaker.

Killigrew enjoys blending his interest in cutting, milling, and drying salvaged and found trees with furniture making to create beautiful objects.

About This Box:

Michael Killigrew's interpretation of the traditional silverware chest combines practicality with grace of line. The curved lid, lovingly hand-carved from a single piece of 2"-thick wood, opens to reveal two stacking trays, each with a manufactured silvercloth rack. The upper tray nestles in rabbets milled on the inside top edge of the lower tray; the lower tray is held in place by four small positioning wedges glued to the inside walls just above the bottom.

The subtle details of this design make an important contribution to its beauty. Killigrew has slightly angled the tops of the sides, so they make a perfect fit with the curved lid; the lid itself is slightly oversize on its long dimension, leaving just enough room for a finger to grip. The paired rails that make up the base are also gently curved, and the tops of the legs, rather than being rounded smooth, are faceted by hand with a chisel, then polished.

PEN/PENCIL BOX & RING BOX

By Elliot Landes

Elliot Landes lives with his wife and two children in the small town of Winters, California. He studied product design at the California College of Arts and Crafts. During his last year of college, he got the idea of turning wood writing instruments, and today is known as one of the country's finest crafters of wooden pens and pencils.

He produces these handmade writing instruments in natural and specially dyed woods from around the world. His current product line includes more than two dozen types of writing instruments and accessories. In the past few years, Elliot has broadened his work with the use of colored woods, powder-coat-black metal finishes, and many lively clip designs.

The Pen/Pencil Box is becoming the centerpiece of his work because of its popularity, and he is introducing other variations using its concept.

About These Boxes:

Elliot Landes has recently branched into box-making with two ingenious designs.

First, he has created the perfect box to store and show off his pen and pencil sets. What's special about this box is that as the lid is opened, the contents of the box are actually lifted up: the box virtually hands you what's inside. The body is a single block of bocote or rosewood with four routed slots. Two are routed long-wise, accommodating the pen and the pencil. The other two are routed cross-wise to allow the pen lifters, which are attached to the back of the lid, to swing up. Assembling the box simply involves gluing the lifters to the lid, drilling the hinge pin holes, and then inserting the pins.

Second, Landes has used the same lifting mechanism in a ring box. The body is a single block of rosewood, with the interior routed out. The ring platform is attached to the back of the lid; using a 1"-diameter flat-bottomed drill bit, Landes drills a shallow depression where the ring will rest, and then fills this space with a slotted velvet pad to hold it. Hinge pin holes are drilled, and pins inserted, just as with the pen box.

Pen and Pencil Box:

Part	Description	Dimensions	Qty.
A	Top	6-1/2 x 1-3/4 x 1/4	1
B	Body	6-1/2 x 1-3/4 x 1-1/2	1
C	Pen lifter	1-3/4 x 3/8 x 1/4	2
D	Hinge pin	1/16 x 1-3/8	2

Ring Box:

Part	Description	Dimensions	Qty.
A	Top	2-1/4 x 1-7/8 x 1/4	1
B	Body	2-1/4 x 1-7/8 x 1-5/8	1
C	Ring platform	1-3/4 x 1-3/8 x 1/4	1
D	Hinge pin	1/16 x 5/8	2

See Diagrams on page 67.

PEN/PENCIL BOX & RING BOX DIAGRAMS

By Elliot Landes

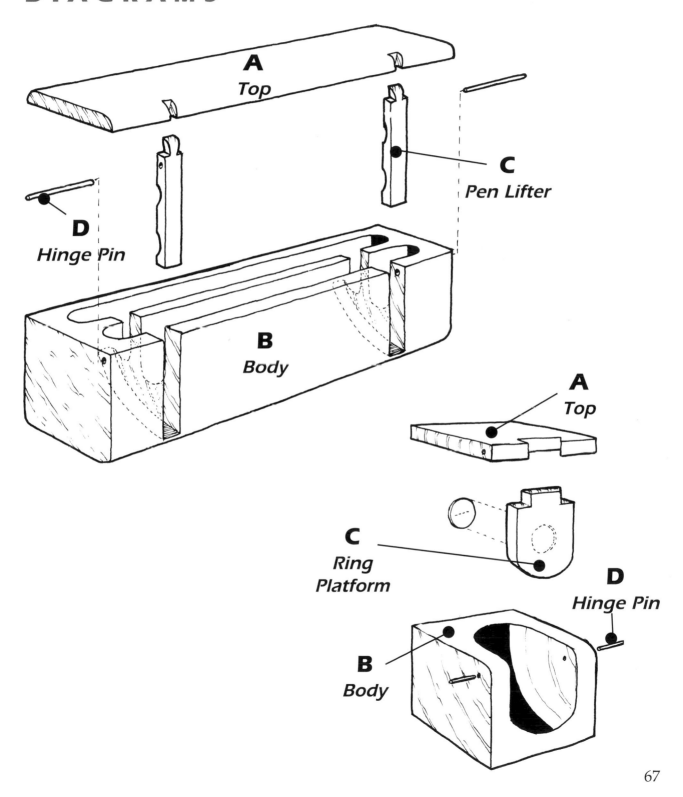

A Top

C Pen Lifter

D Hinge Pin

B Body

A Top

C Ring Platform

D Hinge Pin

B Body

MR. SWEETS

By Kevin Lasher

Currently based in Texas, Kevin Lasher's first exposure to woodworking was through his father's home woodshop. From an early age, Kevin showed an uncommon ability to build pieces that contained a balance of form, function, and design.

Lasher's chose to study Mechanical Engineering at Ohio State University. After graduation he continued to concentrate his energies on engineering, but his passion remained for woodworking. In 1990 he decided to leave the corporate world and start his own woodworking business.

Since that time, Lasher has participated in numerous art and craft shows and his pieces can be found at galleries nationwide. His designs have won widespread acclaim, including a Merit Award from the Memorial Art Gallery in Rochester, New York.

Lasher's philosophy is to let the beauty of the wood dictate styling. Simplicity of form and unencumbered dedication to function give each piece a feeling of solidity and craftsmanship.

About This Box:

Despite their technical sophistication, Kevin Lasher's designs preserve a sense of fun and revel in playfulness. Under the jaunty cap, this purpleheart and satinwood gentleman has a head full of candies, which his nose dispenses one at a time. After bouncing off his mouth, each piece finds its own chattering path on its way through the forest of tumble sticks to his feet, and the child's waiting hand.

Part	Description	Dimensions	Qty.
A	Cap	5-3/4 x 3-1/4 x 1-3/4	1
B	Cap brim	5-1/4 x 5 x 1/4	1
C	Positioning dowel	1-1/2 diameter x 1/2	1
D	Forehead	5-3/4 x 3-1/4 x 13/16	1
E	Cheek	4-1/2 x 3-1/4 x 13/16	2
F	Eye	2 x 1-5/8 x 1-1/4	2
G	Pupil	5/8" diameter x 1/2	2
H	Dispenser end cap	2" diameter x 3/4	2
J	Dispenser dowel	1-3/4 diameter x 7	1
K	Mouth	1-1/8 diameter x 2	1
L	Shoulder	3-1/4 x 3 x 13/16	2
LL	Side	18-1/2 x 3-1/4 x 13/16	2
M	Arm	10-1/2 x 3-5/8 x 13/16	2
N	Back	24 x 8-1/4 x 1/2	1
O	Tumble sticks, dowels	1/8 x 2 and 1/4 x 2	170
P	Acrylic sheet front	24 x 8-1/4 x 1/8	1
Q	Feet	8-1/4 x 4-1/8 x 13/16	1
R	Leg separator	7-1/2 x 1-1/2 x 13/16	1
S	Base	14-1/2 x 6-1/2 x 1-3/4	1
T	Angle block	7 x 2 x 2	1

See Diagrams on pages 70 and 71.

MR. SWEETS DIAGRAM: 1 of 2

By Kevin Lasher

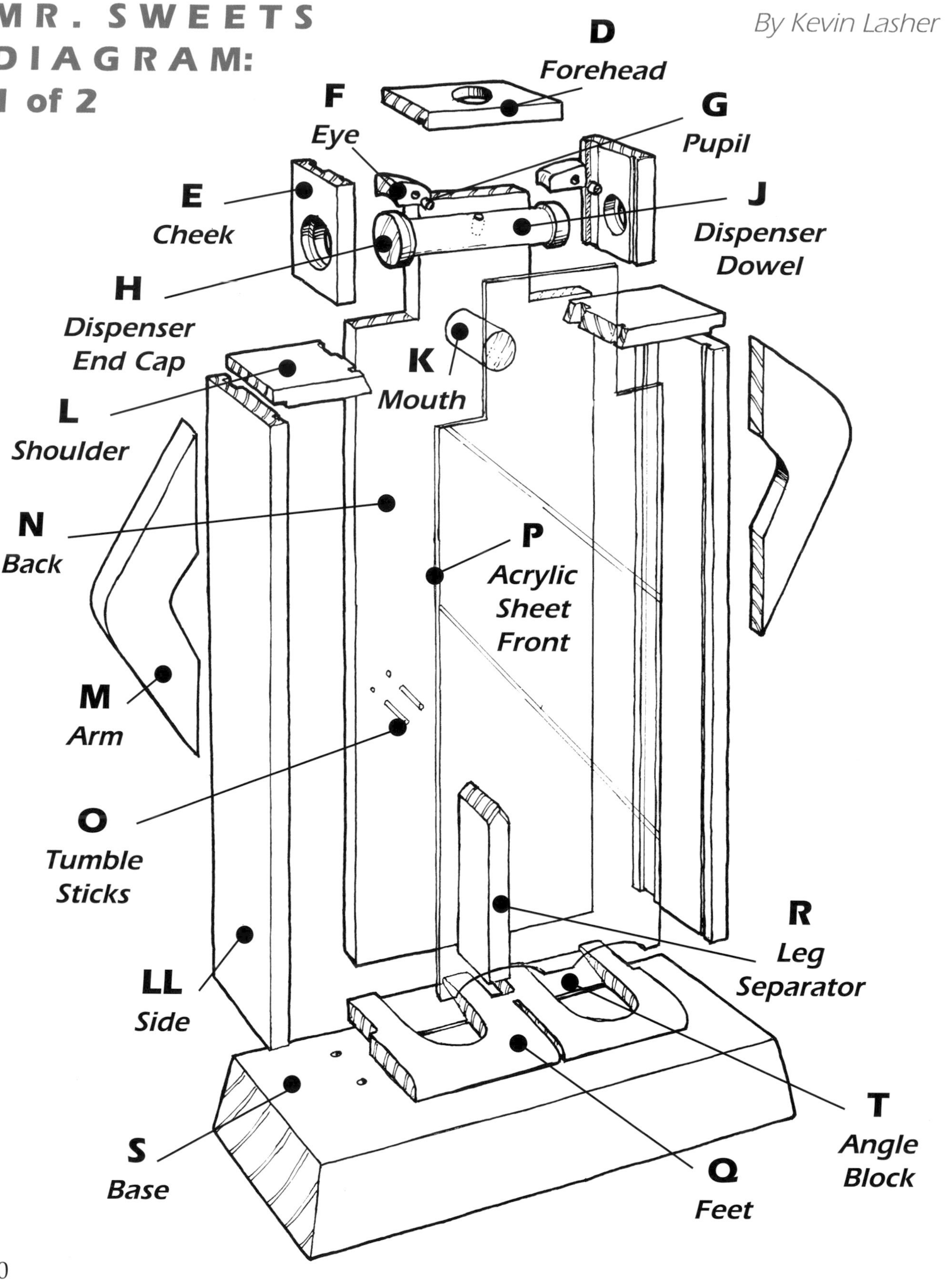
D
Forehead
F
Eye
G
Pupil
E
Cheek
J
Dispenser
Dowel
H
Dispenser
End Cap
K
Mouth
L
Shoulder
N
Back
P
Acrylic
Sheet
Front
M
Arm
O
Tumble
Sticks
LL
Side
R
Leg
Separator
T
Angle
Block
S
Base
Q
Feet

By Kevin Lasher

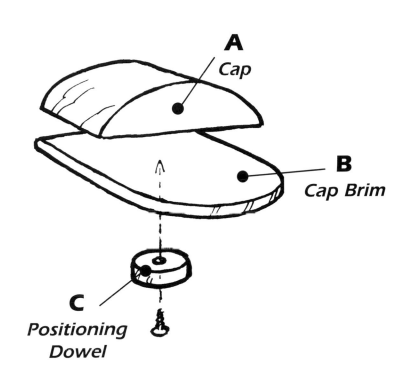

A Cap

B Cap Brim

C Positioning Dowel

WALL-HANGING BOX
By Po Shun Leong

About This Box:
Po Shun Leong's training as an architect is clearly evident in this wall-hanging box made of exotic woods including ebony and pernambuco, as well as familiar ones, like cherry and maple, with touches of gold leaf. Dispersed throughout the complex cityscape are a total of 24 drawers and three compartments.

Po Shun Leong is a California artist who creates architecturally inspired wooden cabinets, jewelry chests, furniture and sculptures which are shown in museums throughout the world.

Born and educated in England, Leong received a scholarship to study in France with Le Corbusier, one of the pioneers of modern architecture. After graduating from the London Architectural Association School with honors, he designed buildings in London, then moved to Mexico, where he lived and designed for 15 years absorbing the indigenous culture.

After moving to Southern California in 1981, Leong started creating cabinets. "My cabinets are really architecture on a smaller scale. I do plans as if they were buildings with floors and a roof."

Leong's works are held in many private collections, including the White House Permanent Craft Collection. Numerous publications have featured articles on his work.

THE HUMIDOR

By Timothy Lydgate

Timothy Lydgate's earliest memories are of the frosty New England woods, where his father and elder brothers chopped and split cord after cord of oak, hickory, and cherry firewood for their living room fireplace. Warmly bundled against the cold, he was lulled to sleep by the rhythmic swish of the two-man saw and, when the crack of splitting logs woke him, his toys were often fragrant chunks of fresh-cut hardwood.

After his formal education, he roamed Europe, Africa, and Asia, absorbing diverse cultural and artistic traditions, and began woodworking after moving to Hawaii in the 1970s.

In the Islands, he rediscovered the pleasure of wood. Beguiling native species put him under their spell, and as he came to know these woods — queenly koa, warm milo, exotic mango — his appreciation for them grew. He developed a passion for figured hardwoods.

He feels that what animates fine craft is a sincere respect for raw materials, and he tries to communicate that respect in his work.

About This Box:

Collectors of fine cigars will appreciate this humidor, which Timothy Lydgate has fashioned from curly koa, mango, and rosewood. Each of the hexagonal sides is made up of seven separate pieces of solid wood, laminated together and then ripped at a 60° angle. Once assembled, the upper rim of the box is edged with thin rosewood strips. After the finish has been applied, a piece of suede trims the bottom, preventing the box from sliding too easily. The interior is lined with thin strips of aromatic cedar.

Beneath its knob, the lid features the same hexagonal construction, with each wedge consisting of five alternating laminate sections of koa, mango, and rosewood. These are made by gluing up a single 19"-long piece of the desired laminate, then cutting six sections at the appropriate angle and gluing them together to form the lid. A 1/4"-thick lid liner of cedar, bordered by another rosewood strip, holds the lid in place.

75

KOA KEEPSAKE

By Tony Lydgate

Judy Dater Photo

America's leading boxmaker, Tony Lydgate is a master craftsman whose inventive designs have earned him a national reputation. Throughout his career, he has been an active advocate for crafts, and is currently a trustee of the American Craft Council, the country's national crafts education and service organization.

He is the author of this book, as well as The Art of Making Elegant Wood Boxes, *also published by Sterling, and his boxes are shown at finer galleries and craft exhibitions throughout the country.*

About This Box:

This box was developed in response to a client's request for a jewelry box featuring drawers and a top section with a lid.

Based on a series of modules, this design has two advantages: module parts can all be milled at the same time, and the modules can be stacked to produce a chest with two, three, or as many drawers as are desired.

The module itself consists of two solid wood sides, with a 1/4" dadoed bottom and a 1/2" flush rabbeted top. Drawer construction is straightforward, and the handles are milled with a 1/8" keel that fits into a saw-kerf slot. The curves on the solid sides of the module are produced using a round-over bit on the router. The lid is made separately, and installed using 1/16" invisible pin hinges as the final step prior to oiling.

This chest is made of spectacular figured Hawaiian koa, with rosewood handles and detailing.

Part	Description	Dimensions	Qty.
A	Lid	11-13/16 x 8-7/8 x 1/2	1
B	Lid border strip	9 x 1/2 x 1/8	2
C	Lid front	11-3/8 x 3 x 1/2	1
D	Handle	5 x 5/8 x 3/8	3
E	Filler block	1/2 x 1/4 x 1/8	2
F	Side	9 x 3 x 13/16	6
G	Lid module, front / back	11-3/8 x 2-1/2 x 1/2	2
H	Lid stop block	2-1/2 x 1-1/2 x 1/4	2
J	Side facing	3 x 13/16 x 1/8	6
K	Top, drawer module	12 x 9 x 1/2	2
L	Top facing	11-1/2 x 1/2 x 1/8	2
M	Drawer front	11-1/2 x 2-1/2 x 1/2	2
N	Drawer bottom	11-1/8 x 8-5/8 x 1/8	2
O	Drawer side	8-7/8 x 2-1/8 x 5/16	4
P	Drawer back	11-1/8 x 2-1/8 x 5/16	2
Q	Module bottom	12-5/8 x 8-3/8 x 1/4	3
R	Module back	13-3/16 x 3 x 1/8	2
S	Hinge pin	1/16 x 3/4	2

See Diagram on page 79.

KOA KEEPSAKE DIAGRAM

By Tony Lydgate

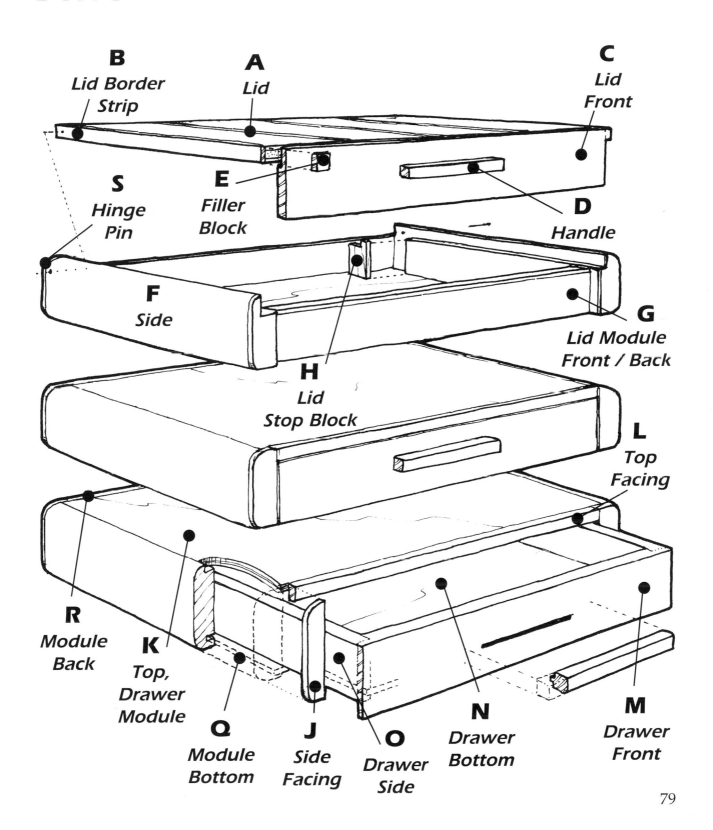

B Lid Border Strip

A Lid

C Lid Front

S Hinge Pin

E Filler Block

D Handle

F Side

G Lid Module Front / Back

H Lid Stop Block

L Top Facing

R Module Back

K Top, Drawer Module

Q Module Bottom

J Side Facing

O Drawer Side

N Drawer Bottom

M Drawer Front

WINGED BOX

By Michael Mode

Michael Mode spent years learning the skills of wood-turning and running a business. Desiring to change and evolve his work, Mode turned for inspiration to his travels through India some 20 years earlier. He was fascinated with the style and aesthetics of the Moguls, whose most well known creation is the Taj Mahal.

The outcome of Mode's evolution is a series of pieces he refers to as "winged vessels." Each differs in size and style, but all have a fluid and graceful quality and a certain alien aspect. The comments often elicited concern oriental temples, undersea creatures (especially manta rays) or spacecraft from other worlds.

Mode works entirely alone. "I am honored to be a conduit for inspirations, and to have the privilege of making my livelihood by their actualization," he says.

About This Box:

While some curved shapes can be produced with a belt sander, the most widely used tool for making curves is the lathe. In his Vermont studio, Michael Mode has become a master at turning breathtakingly delicate forms. In his latest experiments, Mode uses the lathe to produce vessels that combine round and rectangular shapes.

The perfectly round lids of these tiny boxes are typical of lathe-turned forms. The bodies of the boxes, however, are rectangles whose lower, curved wing-like shapes seem to float like undersea creatures. Mode rough-turns these forms while the wood is green, then allows it to dry before re-mounting them on the lathe for the final shaping, sanding, and polishing. Rosewood, burls, and highly figured woods are ideal for this project.

Part	Description	Dimensions	Qty.
A	Lid	2-3/8 x 3/4	1
B	Body	2-3/4 x 3 x 1-1/8	1

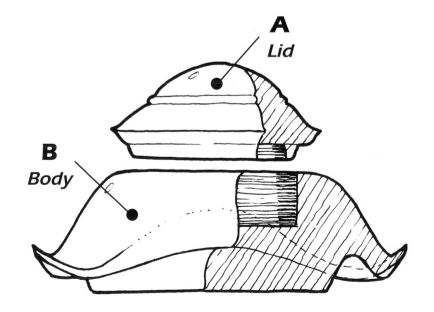

A *Lid*

B *Body*

WINGED VESSEL

By Michael Mode

About This Box:

For a number of years, Michael Mode's interest in form has led him on a unique quest. "I've been trying to discover techniques for creating shapes that don't seem as if they could possibly have been made on a lathe," Mode observes. "I'm fascinated with shapes that appear bent, and that nest in matching curves. Grace, balance, and proportion are the aspects I'm concerned with in developing my vessels, and with this latest winged type of critter, I believe I'm finally getting it!"

DRESS-SHIRT BOX

By Pamela Morin

Michael Keenan Photo

Pamela Morin is an accomplished designer and craftsperson in many areas: graphic design, jewelry, accessories, furniture, and gifts. Her creations can be found in hundreds of galleries, museums, and private collections all over the world. She has a B.S. from Skidmore College, and an MFA from the San Francisco Art Institute, where she was awarded the Robert Fried Memorial Award for outstanding achievement in printmaking. All her work is graphic, bold, exhilarating, amusing, and full of color.

Morin has a vast collection of folk art, from which she draws her inspiration. In 1983, she founded Contemporary Primitives, a company in upstate New York that makes gift products and children's items. The company unites her love of primitive and folk art with her passion for bold color and irreverent humor.

Morin's work has been published in such magazines as House Beautiful, New York Magazine *and* Metropolitan Home *as well as major newspapers in New York, Chicago, San Francisco, and Dallas.*

About This Box:

Pamela Morin thinks boxes should be fun, and her designs celebrate the delights of the everyday.

This Dress-Shirt Box in zebrawood, walnut, maple, and vermillion, which hangs on the wall, provides a special storage compartment for bow ties, cuff links, or anything else that needs to be kept handy.

The curved forms are band-sawed, and their edges given final shaping on the belt sander.

Part	Description	Dimensions	Qty.
A	Front	14-1/2 x 8-1/4 x 1/2	1
B	Door	5-1/2 x 3-3/4 x 1/2	1
C	Box side	7 x 3 x 1/2	2
D	Box side	4 x 3 x 1/2	2
E	Back	6 x 4-1/2 x 1/4	1
F	Dowel	3/4 x 1/4	8
G	Bow tie	3-3/4 x 2 x 1/4	1
H	Shirt collar	3-3/4 x 2-1/4 x 1/4	2
J	Neck	3 x 4-1/2 x 1/4	1
K	Shirt button	3/8 x 1/4	2
L	Door stop	1/2 x 1/2 x 1/4	1
M	Knob	3/4 x 1/2	1
N	Hinge	1 x 1-1/4	2

See Diagram on page 86.

DRESS-SHIRT BOX DIAGRAM

By Pamela Morin

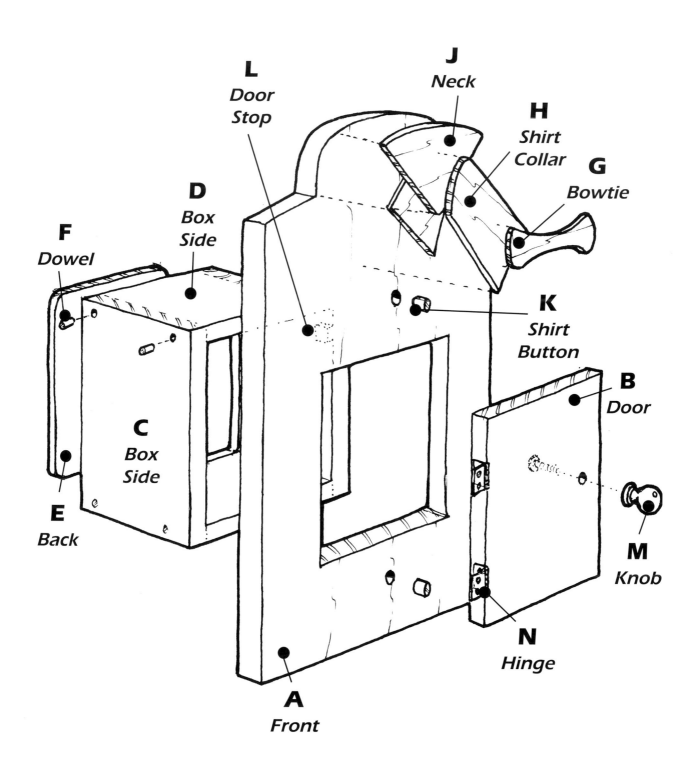

L Door Stop

J Neck

H Shirt Collar

G Bowtie

D Box Side

F Dowel

C Box Side

E Back

K Shirt Button

B Door

M Knob

N Hinge

A Front

BUSINESS CARD BOX DIAGRAM

By Jay and Janet O'Rourke

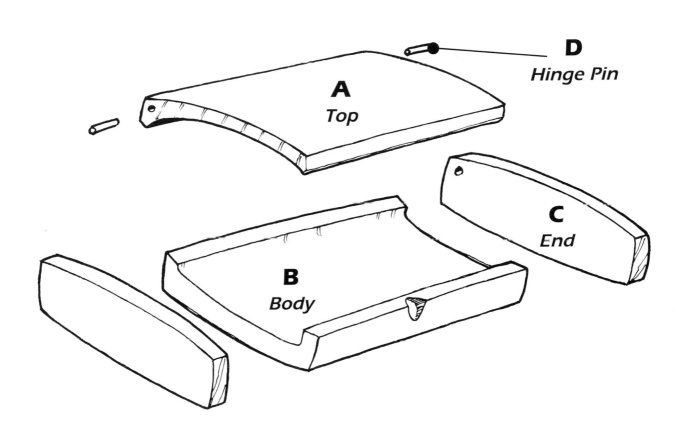

D
Hinge Pin

A
Top

C
End

B
Body

BUSINESS CARD BOX

By Jay and Janet O'Rourke

Jay and Janet O'Rourke combine their talents to operate a woodcraft company, Jay O'Boxes of Oregon, which specializes in unique boxes cut from hand-selected pieces of wood. The beauty of the woods they use—pink ivory, cocobolo, African blackwood, wenge, ebony—makes each box an individual creation.

Their pieces have been exhibited in shows and galleries across the country, including A Celebration of the Creative Works of the Hand; the White House Christmas Tree in 1993, and the Sausalito Art Festival, California, where they won a first-place woodworking award in 1994. They have been published in various books and magazines, including a feature article in American Craft Magazine *in 1994.*

The Pyramid Box shown on page 90 came to the O'Rourkes as a "wish box" design, because they would love to travel to the Mayan and Egyptian pyramids. "They hold a special place in our hearts and dreams," she says.

About This Box:

Jay and Janet O'Rourke are masters at the art of transforming small pieces of intensely colored natural hardwood into gem-like boxes that are as practical as they are irresistible.

This carrying case for business cards begins as only two pieces of wood. From a single block, the lid and body of the box are first cut out on the band saw. A sharp, fine-toothed blade produces a cut so smooth that the interior surfaces do not require any additional sanding. The two ends are cut from a second block of contrasting wood, drilled for the hinge pins along with the lid, and then glued on with the hinge pins in place, so that these are not visible from the outside. The exterior is then carefully shaped and polished, including a final buffing with jewelers' rouge, and the interior is lined with spray flocking.

Part	Description	Dimensions	Qty.
A	Top	3-3/4 x 2-3/4 x 1/4	1
B	Body	3-3/4 x 2-3/4 x 3/4	1
C	End	2-3/4 x 1 x 1/4	2
D	Hinge pin	1/16 x 3/8	2

See Diagram on page 87.

PYRAMID BOX

By Jay and Janet O'Rourke

About This Box:

The boxmaking style of Jay and Janet O'Rourke is characterized by powerful forms, intense colors, gleaming surfaces, and intricate mechanisms. These appear in their simplest designs, like the Business Card Box on page 88, as well as in the dazzling presence of this "Pyramid Box."

Based on the form of an ancient Mayan temple, the O'Rourkes made the body of this box from wenge. The drawer fronts are snakewood, with ebony pulls. African blackwood is used for the legs and the balls, which are covered in 22-carat gold leaf.

POSSIBLE BOX

By David and Kim Okrant

David Okrant had worked as a carpenter in his native Connecticut, and years of going to where the jobs were eventually led him across the country to the coast of northern California, where he met Kim. "I learned two important things about myself during my carpentry days," David recalls. "First, I like the physical, tactile quality of making things with my hands. And second, I like to be able to stand back at the end of the day and see what I've accomplished."

Kim has always been fascinated by the traditional goldsmith's art of lost-wax casting, with its gleaming, silken surfaces, and she studied jewelry making to learn what it takes to produce them.

David found a redwood burl in the backyard and experimented with ways to cut it into box parts. After assembly, Kim's finishing touches made the boxes look so good that the couple decided to take a booth at a local crafts fair. To their surprise and delight, people lined up to buy their work. Since that humble beginning, their pieces have been exhibited in galleries coast to coast.

About This Box:

These hinged boxes by David and Kim Okrant show the beauty that can be attained by keeping a design utterly simple. In the absence of any distracting visual complications, the eye is free to enjoy the satisfying proportions of the Okrants' work, and the way they have shown the natural qualities of the wood at their best.

The black wood is ebonized walnut, which Kim and David began using several years ago as a substitute for true ebony. The lids are made from figured walnut, bird's-eye maple, redwood burl, and other visually striking woods.

CEREMONIAL VESSEL CIRCA 2535 A.D.

By Jonathan Pressler

Jonathan Pressler makes furniture and accessories that reflect his commitment to high style, functional utility, and superior craftsmanship. He constantly strives to explore new media, expand his technical repertoire, and incorporate elements from a variety of design traditions.

Pressler holds a B.A. from Hampshire College and a Ph.D. from the Massachusetts Institute of Technology. For nine years he was a professor, but he found himself increasingly dissatisfied with professional academic life.

Unsure of what he wanted to do, but possessing an interest in furniture making, he studied woodworking and furniture design at the Rochester Institute of Technology's School for American Crafts. He graduated with honors in 1991 and went on to open his own studio.

Pressler's work has been exhibited in both art and craft galleries. Photographs of his furniture have been featured in Woodwork *magazine and* Fine Woodworking's *Design Book Six. He works in upstate New York.*

By making the actual container in this design small compared to the base that supports it, Jonathan Pressler has dramatized his box, while emphasizing — almost sanctifying — the importance of its contents. This is another project in which fine hardwood is used in conjunction with both related and unrelated materials: plywood, sheet aluminum, and colored acrylic rod.

The legs, 3/4" plywood faced on both sides with purpleheart veneer, are set on a turned base of built-up plywood, covered with a thin sheet of aluminum; the base is divided into quadrants by two rosewood strips, with a short section of 3/8" day-glo green acrylic rod at their intersection. Atop the legs, another turned section of built-up plywood forms the body of the box, its upper rim topped by an octagon repeating the plywood/aluminum/rosewood/acrylic theme of the base. The lift-off lid is a single massive turning of purpleheart, with a carved maple handle.

Part	Description	Dimensions	Qty.
A	Handle	5 x 2-3/4 x 3/4	1
B	Lid	7-3/8 diameter x 1-3/4	1
C	Upper rim	9-3/4 octagon x 3/4	1
D	Bowl	11-3/4 diameter x 2	1
E	Dowel	1/4 x 1/2	4
F	Leg	35-1/4 x 12 x 3/4	2
G	Base	12 diameter x 2-1/4	1
H	Wood inlay strip, rim	2 x 1/4 x 1/16	8
J	Wood inlay strip, base	1/16 x 1/4 x 11	2
K	Acrylic rod detailing	1/4 diameter x 1/4	16
L	Aluminum sheet	9-3/4 octagon x 1/16	1
		11" circle	1

See Diagram on page 97.

CEREMONIAL VESSEL
CIRCA 2535 A.D.
DIAGRAM

By Jonathan Pressler

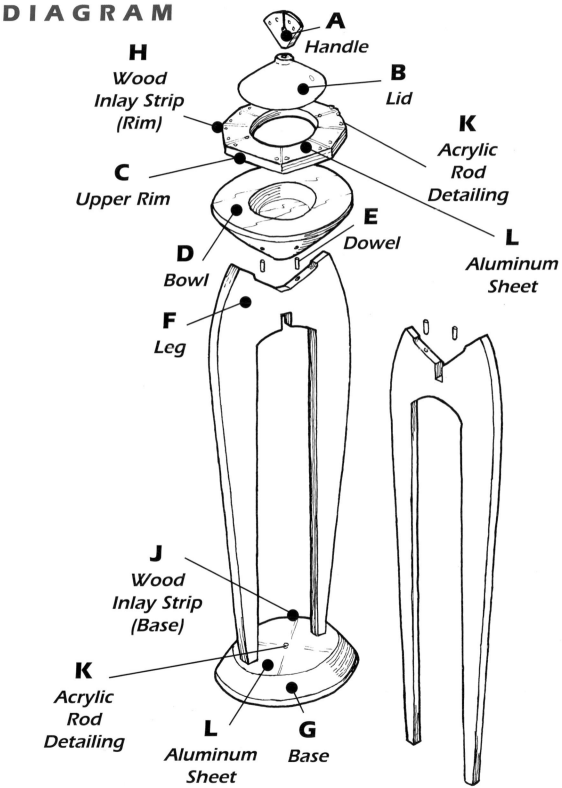

A Handle

H Wood Inlay Strip (Rim)

B Lid

K Acrylic Rod Detailing

C Upper Rim

L Aluminum Sheet

D Bowl

E Dowel

F Leg

J Wood Inlay Strip (Base)

K Acrylic Rod Detailing

L Aluminum Sheet

G Base

LAP DESK

By Rick Rinehart

Rick Rinehart grew up in South Dakota and, at an early age, remembers his grandfather being handy with his hands. This inspired Rinehart to pursue woodworking and he eventually studied woodworking and sculpture at the University of South Dakota. One teacher in particular, Mr. Packard, helped Rinehart appreciate a certain level of craftsmanship that remains with him today.

His livelihood is being a cabinetmaker and making custom furniture, but making small wooden boxes is a sideline business that he enjoys as well.

About This Box:

As a boy growing up in South Dakota, one of Rick Rinehart's favorite objects was an antique rosewood lap desk that had belonged to his great-grandfather. When he became a professional cabinetmaker, reinterpreting that antique designs was one of his first projects.

Rinehart's design uses a combination of solid wood and wood veneer, with purpleheart and lacewood. The veneered parts are laid up on 1/2" medium-density particleboard, which provides a stable substrate for the veneer. A tray at the rear of the box provides storage space for writing instruments, and the space under the upper writing surface, which is hinged, holds paper and envelopes. Leather or various types of cloth or felt can be used to cover the writing surface; Rinehart selected a thin, but durable, blue pigskin.

Part	Description	Dimensions	Qty.
A	Upper writing surface	13 x 7-3/8 x 9/16	1
B	Hinged lid, rear	14-1/8 x 4-1/4 x 9/16	1
C	Hinged lid, front	14-1/16 x 7-3/8 x 9/16	1
D	Side	11-5/8 x 3-5/8 x 1/2	2
E	Back	14-1/8 x 3-5/8 x 1/2	1
F	Front	14-1/8 x 2-1/16 x 1/2	1
G	Bottom	13-1/2 x 11 x 1/4	1
H	Support ledge	10-5/8 x 2-7/8 x 1/8	2
J	Tray side	13 x 1-1/2 x 1/4	2
K	Tray side	3-7/8 x 1-1/2 x 1/4	2
L	Tray bottom	12-3/4 x 3-5/8 x 1/8	1
M	Tray divider	3-5/8 x 1-3/8 x 1/4	2
N	Brass hinge	1 x 1-1/2	4
O	Brass hinge	1/2 x 6	2
P	Leather writing surface	11-1/2 x 14	1

See Diagram on page 101.

LAP DESK DIAGRAM

By Rick Rinehart

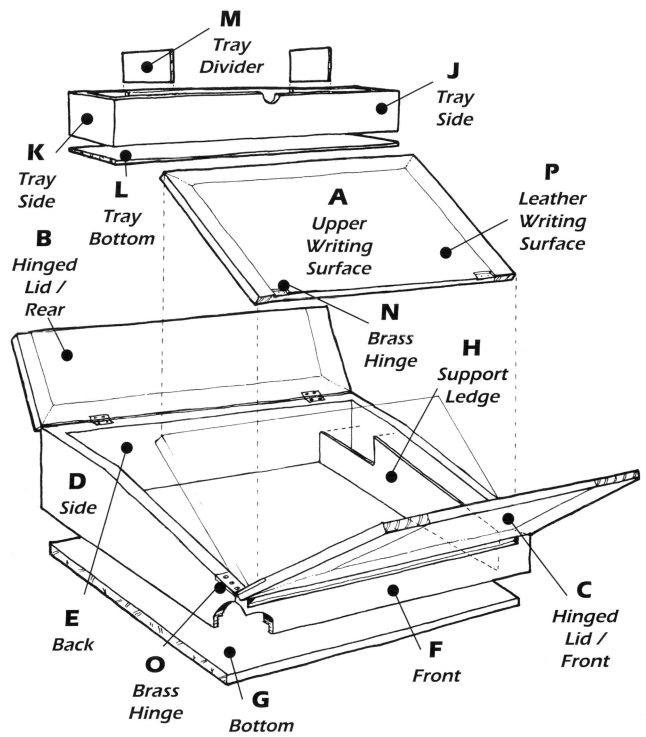

M Tray Divider

J Tray Side

K Tray Side

L Tray Bottom

A Upper Writing Surface

P Leather Writing Surface

B Hinged Lid / Rear

N Brass Hinge

H Support Ledge

D Side

C Hinged Lid / Front

E Back

O Brass Hinge

G Bottom

F Front

PUZZLE BOXES

By Larissa Scott

Larissa Cooper and Scott Dworkin, who call their partnership "Larissa Scott," are the leading American designers of their generation in reviving the puzzle box.

Scott is an art school gruduate, with degrees in both fine art and industrial design, while Larissa was trained in antique restoration.

This unique compatibility has led them to be able to make anything that they can imagine in their California studio.

Larissa Scott's puzzle boxes reflect their combination of creativity and technical expertise. Once the key to each box is discovered and removed, the viewer is delighted by a seemingly endless series of nested and interlocking drawers, boxes, and compartments. Scott and Larissa's technical skill is especially evident on close examination: it is often impossible to determine how the box could possibly have been fabricated.

"This is only the beginning of where I want our work to go," says Scott. "We just got our new band saw — wait till you see what we can do now!"

About These Boxes:

Larissa Cooper and Scott Dworkin have found the perfect way to combine their love of nature with their enthusiasm for the whimsical: they have revived the lost art of the puzzle box.

These boxes operate on the principle of the key, a small piece of wood whose shape interlocks with the body. The box cannot be opened until the key is removed. In many of these designs, the key becomes an integral design element, such as a fish in a shark's mouth. In some, the key is deliberately hidden, and discovering how to open the box can become a fascinating challenge. Inside is a marvellous collection of irregularly shaped compartments and drawers. Since all of these also interlock, the box can be explored only by following the proper sequence.

Each box starts out as a single block of wood. Using the band saw, the bottom of the block is carefully sliced off, and the key cut out. No two boxes are alike, and Larissa and Scott fashion each interior as the spirit moves them, often creating as many as a dozen tiny boxes within drawers within compartments. For all of these, the same process is followed: the bottom is sliced off, the form is band-sawed, then the bottom is glued back on. Finally, each part is lined with flocking and polished.

THE HUNTER &
THE WINGED CHEST

By Jeff and Katrina Seaton

"Collaborating with another artist is always interesting, particularly when he's your husband," Katrina Seaton observes. "Jeff and I have found the best way to combine our talents: we each make a contribution, and yet there's more to the finished piece than either of us could create alone." Travelling and conversation have provided the inspiration for most of the Seaton's design ideas.

Before they met, Katrina was a painter and stained-glass maker, but Jeff has always been a woodworker. "From the day I first happened on a freshly cut redwood burl," he says, "I've known that woodwork was my calling."

The Seatons love the intense color and grain of natural hardwoods, and are concerned that this renewable resource be harvested in a way that preserves forest ecology. This prompts them to get their raw materials only from suppliers who practice responsible forest management.

About These Boxes:

Jeff and Katrina Seaton have designed a series of boxes that have the aura of mystical vessels.

The Hunter has a top of ebony and sea tortoise shell, found on the beach near their Santa Barbara home. The body of the box is walnut burl, and the woods in the lid are chak-ticote, pernambuco, purple-heart, and cocobolo. The lid opens to reveal a 12"-deep compartment. Attached to the pernambuco face with gold bolts, a cast copper sculpture represents an anthropomorphic hunter.

The Winged Chest (shown on pages 114 and 115) consists of a padouk body below a pair of book-matched texturized ebony wings, attached with sterling silver tubes. Dyed raffia tufts serve as an accent, and the same material is woven into a band around the bottom. The interior is lined with suede.

DIAMOND-PLATE JEWELRY BOX

By Brad Smith

Brad Smith's interest in woodworking started in high school and followed him to the Rochester Institute of Technology School for American Craftsmen, where he studied furniture design.

In 1980, Smith set up shop on his father's Pennsylvania farm. His business, Bradford Woodworking, began with a line of kitchen tools and accessories. In 1987 he launched into furniture making, in which he incorporates some of the "farm life" around him, using pitchforks, axe handles, and disc blades as elements in his furniture.

Smith owns an unusual piece of equipment called an axe-handle lathe, which is about 100 years old. He uses it to make furniture legs and lamp and bed posts. The machine creates an interesting surface texture which Smith emphasizes by painting and then sanding through the paint. The textured sides of the jewelry box shown were made on this lathe.

About This Box:

Combining wood with materials such as metal, acrylic, glass, vinyl, fiber, and stone is one of the most interesting trends in box-making today. Boxes have always been mixed-media objects, employing metal for hinges and hardware, fiber linings, mirrors, and glass. Recently, however, leading woodworkers like Brad Smith have made some startling innovations. For this jewelry box, Smith fashions a lid from diamond-plate steel, includes a bevelled mirror, and uses paint to create a striking striped pattern on traditional cherry wood.

The body is a box within a box: the curved cherry exterior surrounds an interior box of 1/2"-thick walnut, finger-jointed for strength. The lid pivots on a steel rod welded to its top surface; the ends of this rod rest on depressions carved in oak hinge supports.

Part	Description	Dimensions	Qty.
A	Lid	11-1/2 x 11-1/2 x 1/4	1
B	Hinge rod	1/2 diameter x 12-3/4	1
C	Bevelled mirror	10-1/2 x 10-1/2	1
D	Tray side	11-5/8 x 7/8 x 5/16	2
E	Tray side	8 x 7/8 x 5/16	2
F	Tray divider	7-11/16 x 3/4 x 5/16	1
G	Tray bottom	11-5/8 x 8 x 1/8	1
H	Box liner	12-5/8 x 3-7/8 x 1/2	4
J	Hinge rod support	11-11/16 x 2-1/8 x 1/2	2
K	Side	15-3/4 x 3-1/4 x 1-5/8	4
L	Bottom	12-1/2 x 12-1/2 x 1/4	1

See Diagrams on page 119.

DIAMOND-PLATE JEWELRY BOX DIAGRAMS

By Brad Smith

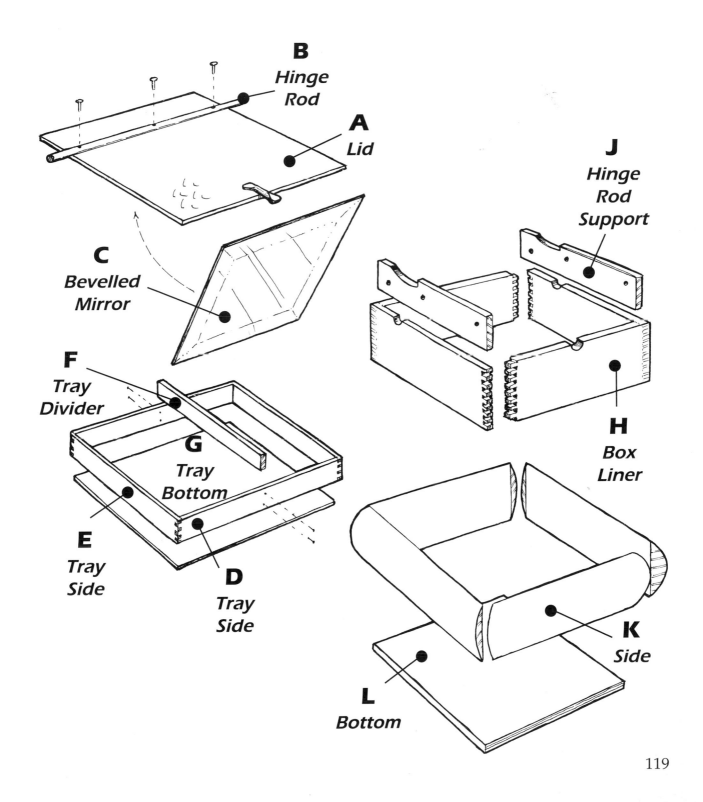

B Hinge Rod

A Lid

C Bevelled Mirror

J Hinge Rod Support

F Tray Divider

G Tray Bottom

E Tray Side

D Tray Side

H Box Liner

K Side

L Bottom

CARVED-LID BOXES

By Ervin Somogyi

Many of the boxmakers featured in this book have been carpenters or cabinetmakers, or made furniture or done other kinds of woodworking at some point in their careers. But only one, Ervin Somogyi of Berkeley, California, is famous as a designer and builder of guitars.

Somogyi (pronounced "So-MAH-dji") is among the most prominent luthiers in the world.

Instruments in the guitar and lute family possess a circular sound hole, traditionally decorated with an inlaid or carved rosette. Somogyi uses his extraordinary skill as a designer and carver to turn this decoration into an art form all its own.

"To make one of these carvings, I start with 1/8"-thick guitar-top wood such as cedar or spruce. Softwoods like these take a clean cut without too much pressure," he says. He uses surgical scalpels for most of his cutting, but it is persistence and elbow grease that get the job done.

Each box lid may contain as many as 3,000 separate cut lines, each of which requires up to 15 individual cutting strokes.

About These Boxes:

Ervin Somogyi brings the precision and skill of a guitar maker to his boxes, giving each a meticulously hand-carved lid.

The box on page 120 has a four interlocking-mosaics inlay ring design, borrowed from the tradition of the Japanese family crest. The design is not painted, nor is it a decal: it's made up of some 16,200 pieces of dyed wood, inlaid into a book-matched piece of solid cedar.

The lid of the box on page 122 is embellished with a Celtic design of intertwined animals, based on a smaller version in the Book of Kells. Somogyi's carving contains over 900 individual lines, each requiring up to 15 cutting strokes.

The lid of the third box contains a marvelously flowing interlaced pattern. Although this is also a Celtic design, it is reminiscent of classical Islamic calligraphy. Artists in both the Islamic and Celtic traditions created designs to reflect a sense of continuity and interconnectedness in the world; Celtic versions tend to be more woven and organic, while Islamic versions are more angular and geometric.

With his exquisite skill, Somogyi has given the hard edges of scalpel-carved wood the fluidity of an artist's brushstrokes.

SCROLL CASE

By Steven Spiro

Steven Spiro was born in Fort Collins, Colorado. He was educated at San Francisco State University and received a B.A. and Advanced Studies Degree in Wood and Furniture Design. He began working with wood in 1971, and since then has exhibited his work at art shows and galleries across the nation.

Spiro's designs are characterized by a powerful sense of form, and a sure instinct for embellishment. As a result, he is viewed by many as the country's leading innovator in wood surface design.

Outside of his Wisconsin studio, Spiro is an active contributor to professional activities for the American Craft Council, as well as a visiting lecturer and artist.

His work is frequently featured in national publications as diverse as The Wall Street Journal, The New York Times, Fine Woodworking, *and* Country Living.

About This Box:

Steven Spiro, a furniture maker based in Wisconsin, set out to explore the idea of a box without four sides, a bottom, and a top. The result was this simple, yet fascinating, case. Its cylindrical form is constructed on the principles of traditional cooperage or barrelmaking.

Curved staves are carved from individual pieces of solid wood, then bevelled on their long edges so they join together perfectly to produce the cylindrical form. The ends of the box are bandsawed and carved from stack-laminated blocks, with Spiro's trademark inlay spiralling over them and across the lid.

For a hinge, Spiro has used a piece of leather, as shown in the drawing. An ingenious key consists of a handle containing a 1/8" dowel. Instead of turning like a conventional key, the dowel is pushed through the circular keyhole; its tip bends back the latch far enough to clear its strike.

Part	Description	Dimensions	Qty.
A	End	13 x 1-3/4	2
B	Foot	10 x 6 x 1-3/4	2
C	Lid	22-3/4 x 3/4	1
D	Bottom	22-3/4 x 6 x 3/4	1
E	String anchor	1/8 x 1/2	4
F	Leather hinge	As required	1
G	Latch	2 x 3/4 x 1/2	1
H	Strike	3/4 x 1/2 x 1	1
J	Key	1-1/2 x 3/4 x 1	1
K	Key dowel	1/8 x 1-1/4	1

See Diagram on page 127.

SCROLL CASE
DIAGRAM

By Steven Spiro

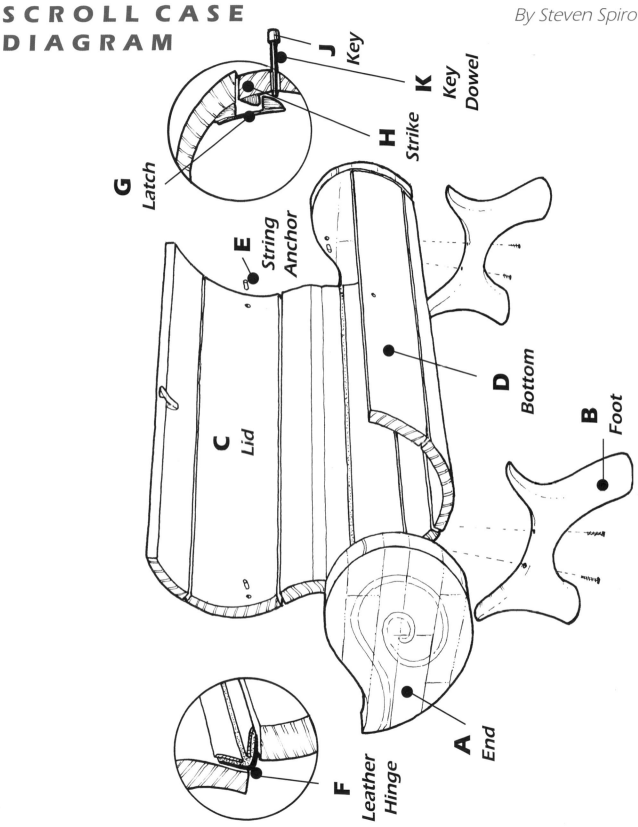

J Key

K Key Dowel

H Strike

G Latch

E String Anchor

C Lid

D Bottom

B Foot

A End

F Leather Hinge

TOWER BOX

By Gary Upton

A California native, Gary Upton attended San Jose State University, studying sculpture crafts and silver fabrication and jewelry. Finding himself incorporating more and more wood into his jewelry pieces, he decided to learn more about woodworking. He attended Anderson Ranch School in Aspen, Colorado, and studied with Arthur (Espenet) Carpenter, Sam Maloof, and John Nyquist.

In 1976, Upton opened his own studio, which is currently located in Grass Valley, California, and where his furniture creations come into being.

His work has been shown in galleries throughout California and published in magazines such as Fine Woodworking, Woodwork, *and* Northern California Home and Garden.

"I find working with stone and wood an experience in the power of contrast. Like the masculine and feminine in all of us, both have distinctive properties that interact and enhance each other. I pursue the balance of these elements through the refinement of form," says Upton.

About This Box:

The sleek but modest exterior of this jewelry box by Gary Upton gives no hint of either how it operates or what it might contain.

Like Steven Spiro with the Scroll Case on page 124, Upton has avoided conventional rectangles, and used instead a curved triangular shape, standing upright. The three legs are carved from solid pieces of teak; the curved door and two sides of the box are walnut veneer laminated onto curved panels.

The door itself is the box: turning on a pivot in the base, it rotates to reveal four storage racks, each made of thin bent ebony and lined with ultrasuede, and each designed to hold a different kind of jewelry.

Part	Description	Dimensions	Qty.
A	Leg	29 x 1-3/4 x 1-3/4	3
B	Top	10 x 7-1/2 x 2	1
C	Bottom	10 x 7-1/2 x 3/4	1
D	Door	19 x 8 x 3/4	1
E	Side	19-1/4 x 7-1/2 x 1/2	2
F	Compartment fronts	9 x 1-1/2 x 1/4	4
G	Pivot		2
H	Compartment bottom	9 x 4 x 1/2	4
J	Bullet catch		4

See Diagram on page 131.

TOWER BOX
DIAGRAM

By Gary Upton

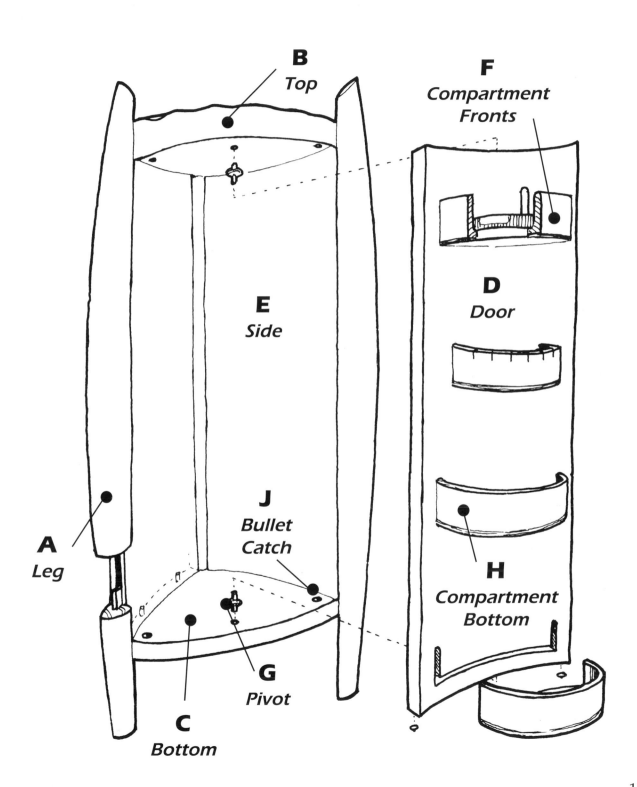

B
Top

F
*Compartment
Fronts*

E
Side

D
Door

J
*Bullet
Catch*

A
Leg

H
*Compartment
Bottom*

G
Pivot

C
Bottom

THREE-DRAWER CHEST

By Gary Upton

About This Box:

In his most recent mixed-media exploration, California woodworker Gary Upton has retained all the elements of an old-fashioned wooden three-drawer chest, but used burnished aluminum and slate instead of wood for legs and top. The result is a design that is both traditional and startlingly modern.

The drawers are made of quilted western maple, constructed in the conventional manner using hidden vertical splines to reinforce the four mitered corners. The drawers run on square ebony rails, set at a 45° angle, which slide in slots dadoed into the drawer sides. The reinforcing splines show as intricate angular details at the corners, where the dado cut reveals them. The rails screw to the tubular aluminum legs, and four turned knobs over machine screws attach the solid slate top. Two of the drawers feature removable jewelry compartments, and the drawer handles are carved ebony.

Part	Description	Dimensions	Qty.
A	Top	17 x 12 x 3/4	1
B	Knob	1" diameter	4
C	Leg	6-1/4 x 2" diameter	4
D	Drawer rail	10-1/2 x 1/2 x 1/2	6
E	Rubber foot	1-3/4 diameter x 1/8	4
F	Drawer front / back	11-1/8 x 1-3/4 x 1/2	6
G	Drawer side	10-1/8 x 1-3/4 x 1/2	6
H	Routed tray	9-1/16 x 5 x 7/8	2
J	Spline	1-3/4 x 1/2 x 1/8	12
K	Drawer bottom	10-5/8 x 9-5/8 x 1/4	3
L	Drawer pull	7/8 x 3/8 diameter	3
M	Tray support	9-1/8 x 5/8 x 1/8	6
N	Drawer stop pins	1/8 diameter x 1/2	6

See Diagram on page 135.

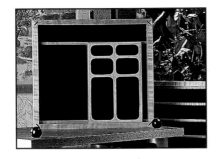

THREE-DRAWER CHEST DIAGRAM

By Gary Upton

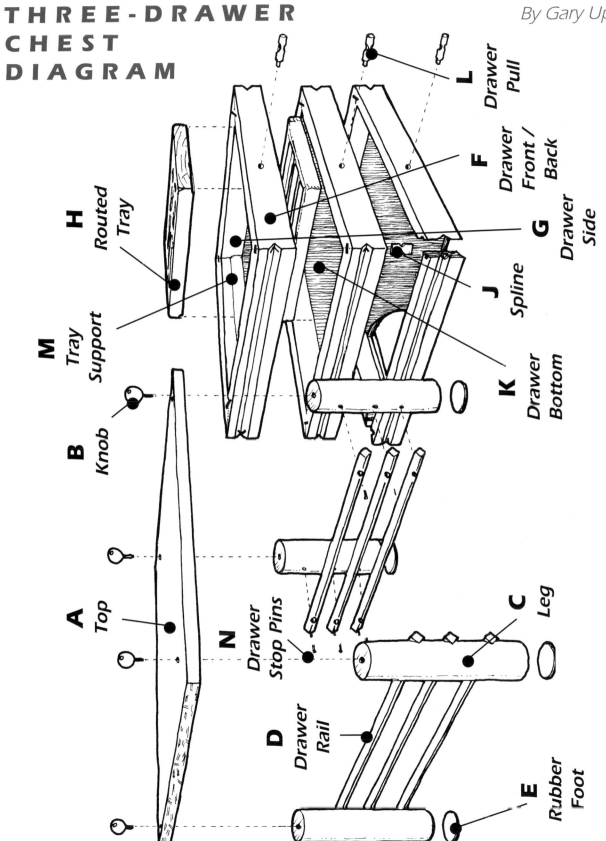

A *Top*

B *Knob*

C *Leg*

D *Drawer Rail*

E *Rubber Foot*

F *Drawer Front / Back*

G *Drawer Side*

H *Routed Tray*

J *Spline*

K *Drawer Bottom*

L *Drawer Pull*

M *Tray Support*

N *Drawer Stop Pins*

ARCHITECTURE BOX

By Phil Weber

Liking to work with his hands led Phil Weber to seek a craft he could both excel at and enjoy. In 1976, Weber discovered woodworking. After taking one or two basic courses, he concentrated his skill on boxmaking, which led to the opening of his own shop in 1982.

Weber and his wife now live and work in Maine — a place where he feels comfortable and creative.

He exhibits his work in many shows, including the prestigious Philadelphia Craft Show, which has accepted his pieces three times and awarded him first prize in 1991. His finely crafted boxes are sold at galleries across the country.

Weber's favorite wood is ebony, not only for its excellent quality, but for the way its black color complements the other woods and metals it is used with, as you will notice in his featured design.

About This Box:

Phil Weber is renowned for his superb craftsmanship as a box-maker, and he does much of his most striking work in ebony, like Architecture Box, featured here. Weber has designed this piece in such a way as to make it appear almost scale-free: although its height is barely 16 inches, it easily suggests a building of 16 storeys.

SURPRISE BOX

By Leon Wiesener

Leon Wiesener taught for 15 years at colleges and universities in the Southeast before resigning in 1981 from the University of Tennessee art department. Wiesener felt that he wasn't being effective as a teacher and that his painting and drafting had become stale. Three years ago, Wiesener found a renewed concern and point of view. Recently building a large glass-blowing studio and producing a one-man show at Tuscullum College in Greeneville, Tennessee, he is happy to be working again.

Wiesener's exhibition and award record is extensive, spanning 30 years. He does free-lance work for Joint Effort Productions, a company which provides scenic services nationally and internationally.

Wiesener emphasizes, "I am not a boxmaker exclusively. I am a painter striving to perfect my art, not necessarily my craft. The ventures into boxmaking reflect my need to hide information so that an effort is required to discover it and also, hopefully, my sense of humor."

About This Box:

Wiesener's mixed-media Surprise Box starts with a deliberately plain cherry body whose lid slides in an angled track. Before applying a coat of varnish, Wiesener decorates the sides of the box with chalk, gold leaf, and paint; he then adds sections of a branch from the same cherry tree.

The blown-glass feet were made by a fellow Tennessee craftsman, Mark Russell. As the lid slides open, a string attached to its underside pulls up the surprise—a lively hand-carved and painted fish with netting for a fin.

METRIC CONVERSION CHART

INCHES TO MILLIMETERS AND CENTIMETERS
MM — Millimeters   CM — Centimeters

INCHES	MM	CM	INCHES	MM	CM	INCHES	MM	CM
1/8	3	0.3	9	229	22.9	30	762	76.2
1/4	6	0.6	10	254	25.4	31	787	78.7
3/8	10	1.0	11	279	27.9	32	813	81.3
1/2	13	1.3	12	305	30.5	33	838	83.8
5/8	16	1.6	13	330	33.0	34	864	86.4
3/4	19	1.9	14	356	35.6	35	889	88.9
7/8	22	2.2	15	381	38.1	36	914	91.4
1	25	2.5	16	406	40.6	37	940	94.0
1-1/4	32	3.2	17	432	43.2	38	965	96.5
1-1/2	38	3.8	18	457	45.7	39	991	99.1
1-3/4	44	4.4	19	483	48.3	40	1016	101.6
2	51	5.1	20	508	50.8	41	1041	104.1
2-1/2	64	6.4	21	533	53.3	42	1067	106.7
3	76	7.6	22	559	55.9	43	1092	109.2
3-1/2	89	8.9	23	584	58.4	44	1118	111.8
4	102	10.2	24	610	61.0	45	1143	114.3
4-1/2	114	11.4	25	635	63.5	46	1168	116.8
5	127	12.7	26	660	66.0	47	1194	119.4
6	152	15.2	27	686	68.6	48	1219	121.9
7	178	17.8	28	711	71.1	49	1245	124.5
8	203	20.3	29	737	73.7	50	1270	127.0

YARDS TO METERS

YDS	METERS	YDS	METERS	YDS	METERS	YDS	METERS	YDS	METERS
1/8	0.11	2-1/8	1.94	4-1/8	3.77	6-1/8	5.60	8-1/8	7.43
1/4	0.23	2-1/4	2.06	4-1/4	3.89	6-1/4	5.72	8-1/4	7.54
3/8	0.34	2-3/8	2.17	4-3/8	4.00	6-3/8	5.83	8-3/8	7.66
1/2	0.46	2-1/2	2.29	4-1/2	4.11	6-1/2	5.94	8-1/2	7.77
5/8	0.57	2-5/8	2.40	4-5/8	4.23	6-5/8	6.06	8-5/8	7.89
3/4	0.69	2-3/4	2.51	4-3/4	4.34	6-3/4	6.17	8-3/4	8.00
7/8	0.80	2-7/8	2.63	4-7/8	4.46	6-7/8	6.29	8-7/8	8.12
1	0.91	3	2.74	5	4.57	7	6.40	9	8.23
1-1/8	1.03	3-1/8	2.86	5-1/8	4.69	7-1/8	6.52	9-1/8	8.34
1-1/4	1.14	3-1/4	2.97	5-1/4	4.80	7-1/4	6.63	9-1/4	8.46
1-3/8	1.26	3-3/8	3.09	5-3/8	4.91	7-3/8	6.74	9-3/8	8.57
1-1/2	1.37	3-1/2	3.20	5-1/2	5.03	7-1/2	6.86	9-1/2	8.69
1-5/8	1.49	3-5/8	3.31	5-5/8	5.14	7-5/8	6.97	9-5/8	8.80
1-3/4	1.60	3-3/4	3.43	5-3/4	5.26	7-3/4	7.09	9-3/4	8.92
1-7/8	1.71	3-7/8	3.54	5-7/8	5.37	7-7/8	7.20	9-7/8	9.03
2	1.83	4	3.66	6	5.49	8	7.32	10	9.14

INDEX

INDEX

SOUNDS OF LANGUAGE

readers

SOUNDS
Around the Clock

By **Bill Martin Jr**
with **Peggy Brogan** and
John Archambault

DLM®

One DLM Park • Allen, Texas 75002

ACKNOWLEDGMENTS

"The End" from NOW WE ARE SIX by A. A. Milne. Copyright 1927 by
E. P. Dutton, renewed 1955 by A. A. Milne. Reprinted by permission of the
publisher, Dutton Children's Books, a division of Penguin Books USA
Inc. By permission also of the Canadian Publishers, McClelland and
Stewart, Toronto.

"Oh My Goodness, Oh My Dear" is the text and art from FATHER FOX'S
PENNYRHYMES by Clyde Watson. Illustrated by Wendy Watson. (Crow-
ell) Text copyright © 1971 by Clyde Watson, Illustrations copyright © 1971
by Wendy Watson. Reprinted by permission of Harper & Row, Publishers,
Inc.

"Who Is Tapping at My Window?" by A. G. Deming is published by
Beckley-Carday Company. Extensive research failed to locate the author/
copyright holder of this work.

WHERE ARE YOU GOING, LITTLE MOUSE? by Robert Kraus, illus-
trated by Jose Aruego and Ariane Dewey. Text copyright © 1986 by Robert
Kraus. Illustrations copyright © 1986 by Jose Aruego and Ariane Dewey.
By permission of Greenwillow Books (A Division of William Morrow and
Company, Inc.)

"Oodles of Noodles" from OODLES OF NOODLES by Lucia & James
Hymes, Jr. © 1964 Addison-Wesley Publishing Co., Inc., Reading, Massachusetts. Reprinted by permission of the publisher.

"When You're Smiling" by Mark Fisher, Joe Goodwin & Larry Shay.
Copyright © 1928 (Renewed 1956) MILLS MUSIC, INC. All rights reserved.
Used by permission.

"So Many Monkeys" from OPEN THE DOOR by Marion Edey (New York:
Scribner's 1949). Reprinted with permission of Charles Scribner's Sons,
an imprint of Macmillan Publishing Company.

"Five Little Monkeys" was first published as "The Monkeys and the
Crocodile" and "Seven Little Tigers" was taken from the longer poem "The
Seven Little Tigers and the Aged Cook." Both are from TIRRA LIRRA
by Laura E. Richards, Little Brown and Company.

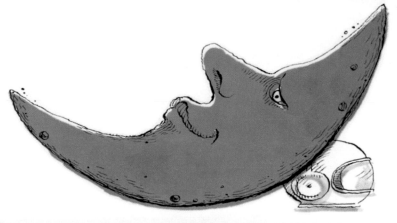

CONTENTS

SOUNDS AROUND THE CLOCK

The End

a poem by A. A. Milne
pictures by Sonia O. Lisker

When I was One,
I had just begun.

When I was Two,
I was nearly new.

15

When I was Three,
I was hardly Me.

18

When I was Four,
I was not much more.

When I was Five,
I was just alive.

But now I am Six,
    I'm as clever as clever.
So I think I'll be six now
    for ever and ever.

Three Little Bugs

in a basket,

Hardly room for two;

One looks like her, one looks like him

And one looks just like you.

an old jingle
art by Ray Barber

As Tommy Snooks and Bessy Brooks
were walking out on Monday,
Said Tommy Snooks to Bessy Brooks,
"Yesterday was Sunday."

a Mother Goose rhyme
drawings by Papas

25

WHO IS TAPPING AT MY WINDOW?

a poem by A. G. Deming
design by Eric Carle

It's not I said the cat.

It's not I said the rat.

 It's not I said the wren.

It's not I said the hen.

 It's not I said the fox.

 It's not I said the ox.

26

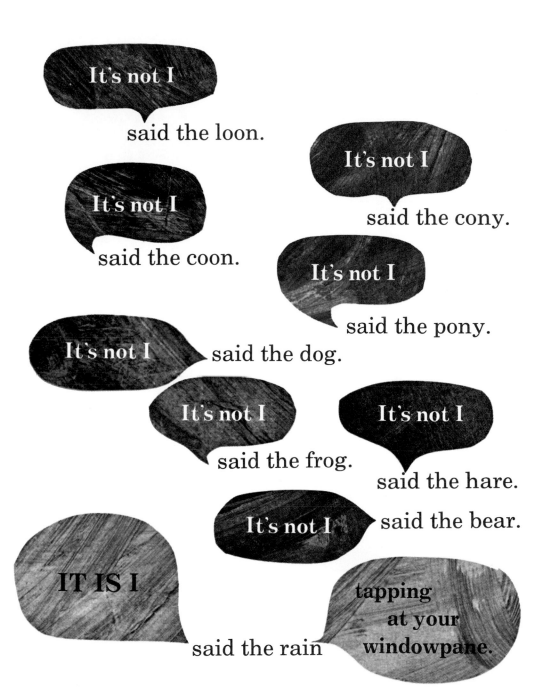

said the loon.

said the coon.

said the cony.

said the pony.

said the dog.

said the frog.

said the hare.

said the bear.

IT IS I said the rain tapping at your windowpane.

Here's a picture for talking about
pear trees in the spring.

painting by Bruce Butte

30

Oh my goodness, oh my dear,
Sassafras & ginger beer,
Chocolate cake & apple punch:
I'm too full to eat my lunch.

a rhyme by Clyde Watson
picture by Wendy Watson

Where Are You Going,
My Little Pig?

"I'm leaving my mother, I'm growing so big!"
  "So big, young pig!
  So young, so big!
  Well, I never before saw a runaway pig!"

a jingle by Thomas Hood
pictures by Aldren Watson

"Where are you going, my little pig?"
"I'm going to the barber's to buy me a wig!"
"A wig, little pig!
A pig in a wig!
Why, whoever before saw a pig in a wig?"

"Where are you going, my little pig?"
"I've got a spade, and I'm going to dig!"
    "To dig, little pig!
     A little pig dig!
   Well, I never before saw a pig that could dig!"

34

"Where are you going, my little pig?"
"Why, I'm off to the ball to dance a fine jig!"
    "A jig, little pig!
    A pig dance a jig!
  Well, I never before saw a pig dance a jig!"

36

Where Are You Going, Little Mouse?

As far from home as I can go.
What of your mother?
What of your father?
What of your sister?
What of your brother?
They don't love me.
They won't miss me.

a story by Robert Kraus
pictures by Jose Aruego and Ariane Dewey

What will you do?
Find a new father who plays with me.
Find a new mother who stays with me.
Find a new brother who isn't mean.
Find a new sister.

Have you found them?
I'm still looking . . .
I miss my mother.
Have you found them?
I'm exploring . . .
I miss my father.

Have you found them?
I'm still searching . . .
I miss my sister.
Have you found them?
I'm still trying . . .
I miss my brother.

It's getting dark.
What will you do?
Make a phone call.
Mother, Father,
please don't worry.
Come and get me.
Hurry, hurry.

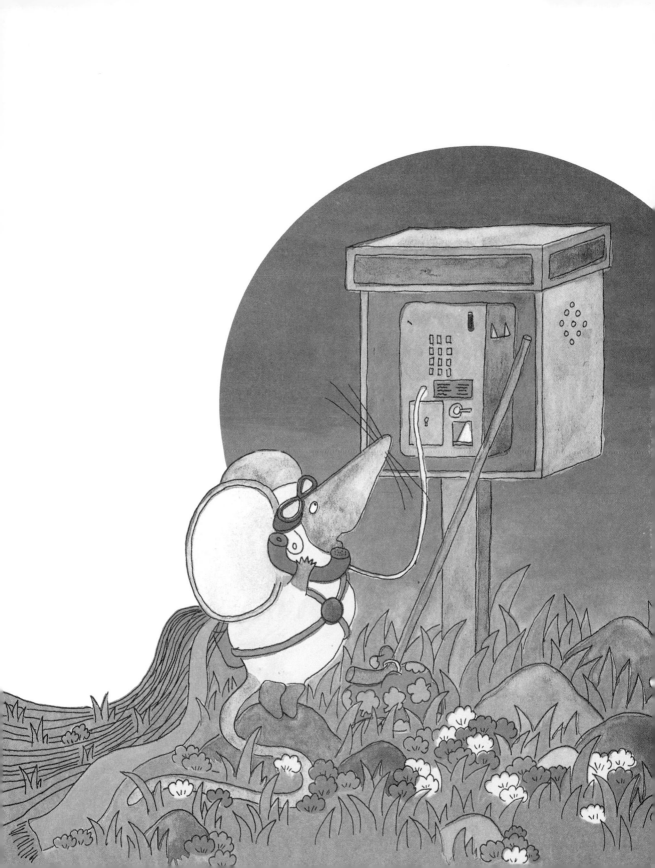

By the way
they kiss and hug me,
I can tell
they really love me.
I love them too.

Here's a picture for talking about trees.

watercolor by LeGreen Richards

Said the kind kangaroo, "Oh, what shall I do?
If I had a cradle, I'd rock it.
But my baby is small so I think after all,
I'll carry her 'round in my pocket."
an old rhyme

L❤VE is something if you give it away

a traditional song
design by Lynda Barber, lettering by Ray Barber

give it away, give it away, L❤VE is something if you give it away, you end up having more. It's just like a magic penny, hold it tight and you won't have any. Lend it, spend it, and you have so many they'll roll all over the floor. So... L❤VE is something if you give it away, you end up having more.

L❤VE is something if you give it away, give it away, give it away, L❤VE is something if you give it away, you end up having more.

Baby Elephant

by Patricia K. Miller and Iran L. Seligman
pictures by Mamoru Funai

This is Ellen.
She is a baby elephant.

She will be a baby
for a long time.
She is three feet tall.
She weighs 200 pounds.

Ellen has small eyes.
She cannot see well.
She has big ears.
She cannot hear well.
Ellen has a long nose.
It is called a trunk.
She uses her trunk in many ways.

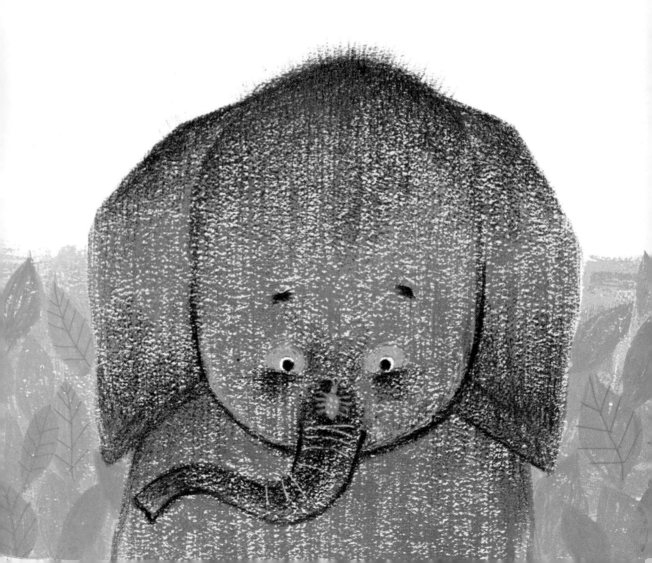

When Ellen holds her trunk in the air,
    she can smell things that are far away.
She picks up food.
She pulls up trees.
She pulls down leaves.
She does all this with her trunk.   53

Ellen has big feet.
She cannot run.
She cannot jump.

But she can walk very fast.

She fills her trunk with water.
She drinks some of the water.
She takes a bath with some of the water.

Ellen likes to play.
She slides down a hill.
She plays in the water.
She hides from her mother.

One day Ellen was hiding
    from her mother.
She fell into a deep hole.
She raised her trunk
    and made a loud noise.

58

Mother came to the hole.
When she saw Ellen,
   she raised her trunk
   and made

 a loud

   noise.

Other elephants came.
The elephants kicked sand into the hole.

They kicked and kicked.
At last the hole was not so deep.
Ellen climbed out of the hole.

Now Ellen is back with the herd.

Is she looking for another place to hide?

Oodles of Noodles

I love noodles. Give me oodles.
Make a mound up to the sun.
Noodles are my favorite foodles.
I eat noodles by the ton.

a poem by Lucia and James L. Hymes, Jr.
picture by Ray Barber

Sometimes I'm not very neat.

So Many Monkeys

Monkey Monkey Moo!
Shall we buy a few?
  Yellow monkeys,
    Purple monkeys,
      Monkeys red and blue.

Be a monkey, do!
Who's a monkey, who?
  He's a monkey,
    She's a monkey,
      You're a monkey, too!

by Marion Edey and Dorothy Grider
picture by Kelly Oechsli

The Purple Cow

by Gelett Burgess

I never saw a Purple Cow,
  I never hope to see one;
But I can tell you, anyhow,
  I'd rather see than be one.

picture by
Robert Jon Antler

Three Potatoes in a Pot,

Take one out and leave two hot.
Two potatoes in a pot,
    Take one out and leave one hot.
One potato in a pot,
    Take it out—
Nothing in the pot.

author unknown
pictures by Kelly Oechsli

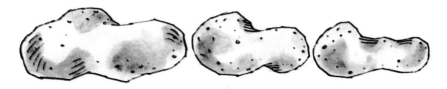

Here's a Picture for Storytelling

picture by George Buckett

This Is My Family

a story by Bill Martin Jr

pictures by Aliki

Hello. My name is Eric.

This is my family.

This is my father.

This is my mother.

This is my brother.

This is my sister

and this is me.

"Mother, is my dog
    a member of our family?"

"Yes, Eric.
Your dog is a member of our family."

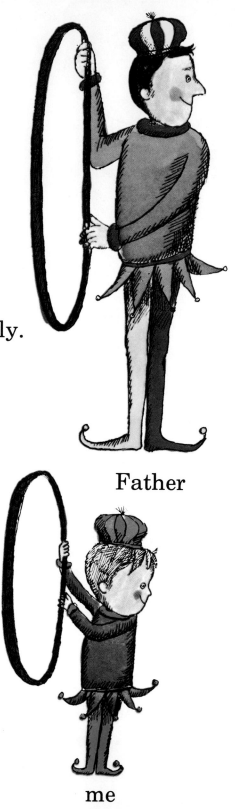

Then, this is my family.

Father

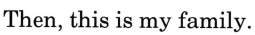

76   Sister   me

Mother   Brother

and my dog.

These are the men in our family.

First, my father. He is a man.

Then my brother.
He is almost a man.

And me.
Someday I will be a man.

These are the women in our family.

First, my mother.
She is a woman.

Then my sister.
She is almost a woman.

Then my dog.
She is a lady dog.

My father is
  the oldest member
  of our family.
My mother is
  next to
  the oldest.

Then my brother.
Then my sister.
Then my dog.
Then me.
I am the
  youngest member
  of our family.

"Mother, does my dog have a dog family?"
"Yes, Eric. Your dog has a dog family.

She has a father.

And a mother.   And three brothers."

"Mother, am I a member
 of my dog's family?"
"No, Eric. You belong to our family.
 This is our family . . .

Father,   Mother,

Brother,   Sister,   your dog,   and you."

My Book

I carry a book

around in my head

of storybook friends

and what they said,

and almost always

they let me play

a part in the story

they're telling today.

by Bill Martin Jr
pictures by Peter Lippman

Seven Little Tigers

they sat them in a row,
Their seven little dinners for to eat;
And each of the troop
Had a little plate of soup,
The effect of which was singularly neat.

a jingle by Laura E. Richards
illustrated by Robert M. Quackenbush

The House That Jack Built

a tale from Mother Goose
pictures by Donald E. Cooke
adapted from old drawings by Frederick Richardson

This is the HOUSE that Jack built.

This is the MALT,
That lay in the house
that Jack built.

94

This is the RAT,
That ate the malt,
That lay in the house
that Jack built.

This is the CAT,
That killed the rat,
That ate the malt,
That lay in the house
　that Jack built.

This is the DOG,
That worried the cat,
That killed the rat,
That ate the malt,
That lay in the house
   that Jack built.

This is the COW
   with the crumpled horn,
That tossed the dog,
That worried the cat,
That killed the rat,
That ate the malt,
That lay in the house
   that Jack built.

This is the MAIDEN all forlorn,
That milked the cow
　　with the crumpled horn,
That tossed the dog,
That worried the cat,
That killed the rat,
That ate the malt,
That lay in the house
　　that Jack built.

This is the MAN all tattered and torn,
That kissed the maiden all forlorn,
That milked the cow
    with the crumpled horn,
That tossed the dog,
That worried the cat,
That killed the rat,
That ate the malt,
That lay
    in the house
    that
    Jack
    built.

This is the PRIEST all shaven and shorn,
That married the man all tattered and torn,
That kissed the maiden all forlorn,
That milked the cow
    with the crumpled horn,
That tossed the dog,
That worried the cat,
That killed the rat,
That ate the malt,
That lay in the house
    that Jack built.

This is the COCK that crowed in the morn,
That waked the priest all shaven and shorn,
That married the man all tattered and torn,
That kissed the maiden all forlorn,
That milked the cow
    with the crumpled horn,
That tossed the dog, that worried the cat,
That killed the rat, that ate the malt,
That lay in the house that Jack built.

This is the FARMER that sowed the corn,
That kept the cock that crowed in the morn,
That waked the priest all shaven and shorn,
That married the man all tattered and torn,
That kissed the maiden all forlorn,
That milked the cow
    with the crumpled horn,
That tossed the dog, that worried the cat,
That killed the rat, that ate the malt,

That lay in the house that Jack built.

Snow Snow Snow

   Come out! Come out in the snow!
Just look at the snow!
   Come out! Come out in the snow!
Do you like the snow
   Yes or no?
Do you like it in your face?
Yes, I like it any place.

by Raphael Conica
photograph by Joel Weltman

Five Little Monkeys
Swinging from a tree;
Teasing Uncle Crocodile,
Merry as can be.
Swinging high, swinging low,
Swinging left and right:
"Dear Uncle Crocodile,
come and take a bite!"

Four little monkeys
Sitting in a tree;
Heads down, tails down,
Dreary as can be.
Weeping loud, weeping low,
Crying to each other:
"Wicked Uncle Crocodile,
 To gobble up our brother!"

by Laura E. Richards
picture by Kelly Oechsli

The Foolies go to school at night
And learn to read by bright moonlight,

by Bill Martin Jr

But when the moon has lost its light,
What foolies read is out of sight.

pictures by Robert J. Lee

When Foolies Go Fishing
the foolies are wishing

they'll catch fat fishes

that match their fat wishes.

by Bill Martin Jr
pictures by Robert J. Lee

The Foolies Had a Picnic
and roasted hot dogs on a stick,

by Bill Martin Jr
pictures by Robert J. Lee

with watermelon for dessert
to wash away the hot dog dirt.

The New Baby Calf

by Edith Newlin Chase
pictures by James Endicott

Buttercup, the cow,
   had a new baby calf,
    a fine baby calf,
     a strong baby calf,
Not strong like his mother
But strong for a calf,
For *this* baby calf was so *new*!

Buttercup licked him
   with her strong warm tongue,
Buttercup washed him
   with her strong warm tongue,
Buttercup brushed him
   with her strong warm tongue,
And the new baby calf *liked that*!

The new baby calf took
  a very little walk,
   a tiny little walk,
    a teeny little walk,
But his long legs wobbled
When he took a little walk,
And the new baby calf fell down.

Buttercup told him
   with a low soft "Moo-oo!"
That he was doing very well
   for one so very new
And she talked very gently,
   as mother cows do,
And the new baby calf *liked that*!

The new baby calf took
another little walk,
a little longer walk,
a little stronger walk,
He walked around his mother
and he found the place to drink.
And the new baby calf liked *that*!

Buttercup told him
   with another low moo
That drinking milk from mother
   was a fine thing to do,
That she had lots of milk for him
   and for the farmer too,
And the new baby calf liked *that*!

121

The new baby calf drank milk every day,
His legs grew so strong
    that he could run and play,
122

He learned to eat grass,
    and then grain and hay,
And the big baby calf grew fat!

Sally and Manda
are two little lizards
Who gobble up flies
   in their two little gizzards.
They live by a toadstool
   near two little hummocks
And crawl all around
   on their two little stomachs.

by Alice B. Campbell
picture by Robert M. Quackenbush

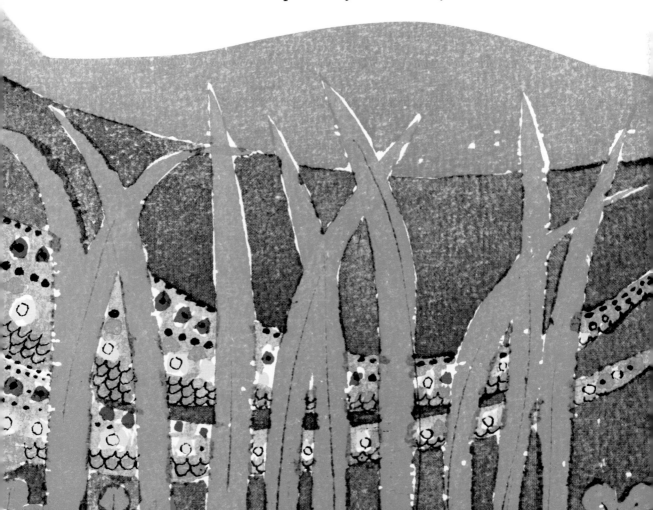

Here's a Picture to Talk About
painting by Ronald Thomason

The Sun Is a Star

by Sune Engelbrektson
pictures by Eric Carle

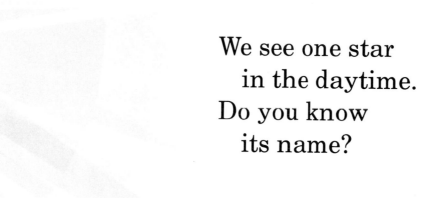

We see one star
in the daytime.
Do you know
its name?

The nighttime stars
   are very far away.
They look like
   tiny points of light.
If our sun
   were as far away
   as the other stars,
   it, too, would look like
   a tiny point of light.

Imagine that
   this flashlight
   is a distant star.
The flashlight
   looks bright
   in the darkness,
   doesn't it?

But now,
   look at the light
   of the flashlight
   in the daytime.
The light cannot be seen
   from far away.
   Do you know why?

Our nearest star, the sun,
   is so bright
   that it keeps us
   from seeing the light
   of the flashlight
   in the daytime.
The sun's brightness
   also keeps us
   from seeing the light
   of other stars
   in the daytime.

Clouds

White sheep, white sheep,
On a blue hill,
When the wind stops
You all stand still.

When the wind blows
You walk away slow.
White sheep, white sheep,
Where do you go?

by Christina G. Rossetti
picture by Gilbert Riswold

135

Sun on the Clover

There's sun on the clover
    And sun on the log,
Sun on the fish pond
    And sun on the frog,

Sun on the honeybee,
  Sun on the crows,
Sun on the wash line
  To dry the clean clothes.

by Louise Fabrice Handcock
picture by Gilbert Riswold

Big Frogs, Little Frogs

by Patricia K. Miller and Iran L. Seligman

pictures by Lee Ames

Big frogs.
Little frogs.
Leaping frogs.
Sleeping frogs.
Swimming frogs
. . . . . and tadpoles.

Listen to the frogs!
Croak!
Croak!
Peep!
Gr-r-ump!

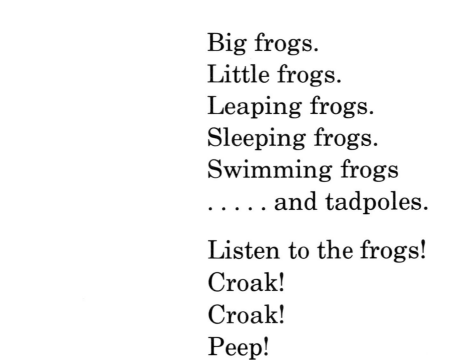

These are frog eggs.
They look like jelly.
Each black dot is
   the beginning of a tadpole.

Tadpoles are baby frogs.
Tadpoles are born from eggs.
They live like fishes in the water.

The tadpoles are growing.
Oh, how fast they grow.
They are turning into frogs.

Tell me, little frog,
what happened to your tail?

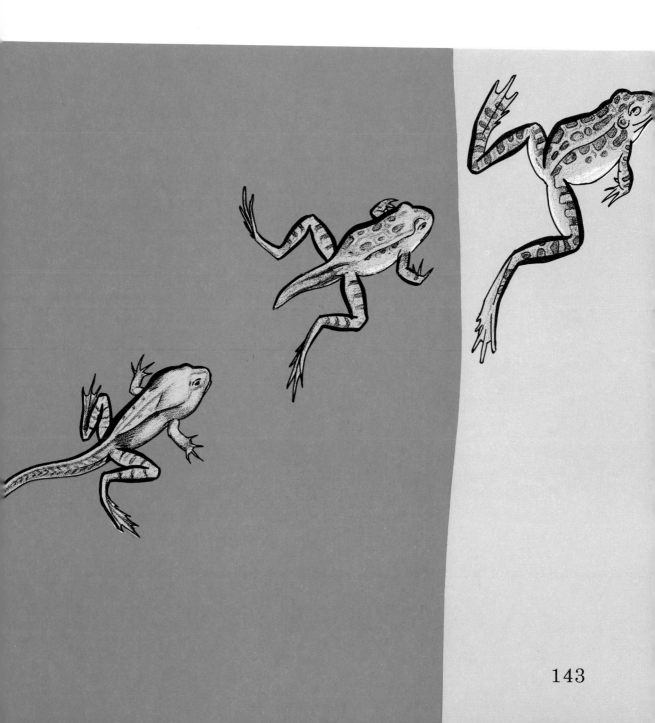

Big frogs.
Little frogs.

Leaping frogs.
Sleeping frogs.

Swimming frogs.
. . . . . And tadpoles.

Listen to the frogs.

Croak!
Croak! Croak!
Peep! Peep! Peep! Peep!

GR-R-UMP!

There was an old man with a beard,

Who said, "It is just as I feared!

Two Owls and a Hen,

Four Larks and a Wren

a limerick by Edward Lear
picture by Kelly Oechsli

Have all built their nests in my beard!"

Summer Morning
Bright and early,
Winds are waking,
Clouds are curly. . . .

Everything
    is rosy, pearly,
Summer morning
    Bright and early.

by Barbara Young
picture by Gilbert Riswold

LOVE SOMEBODY,

LOVE SOMEBODY,

LOVE SOMEBODY,

AND I HOPE SOMEBODY

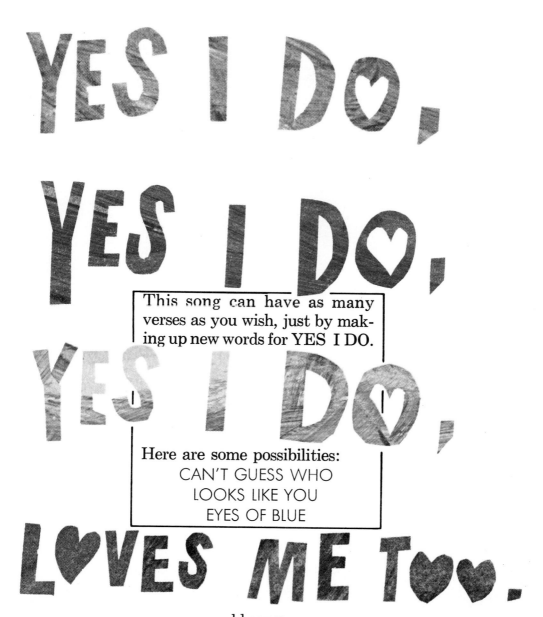

YES I DO,
YES I DO,
YES I DO,
LOVES ME TOO.

This song can have as many verses as you wish, just by making up new words for YES I DO.

Here are some possibilities:
CAN'T GUESS WHO
LOOKS LIKE YOU
EYES OF BLUE

an old song
handlettering by Eric Carle

a song by Mark Fisher, John Goodwin, and Larry Shay
pictures by Sonia O. Lisker

When You're Smiling

When you're smiling,
The whole world smiles with you,

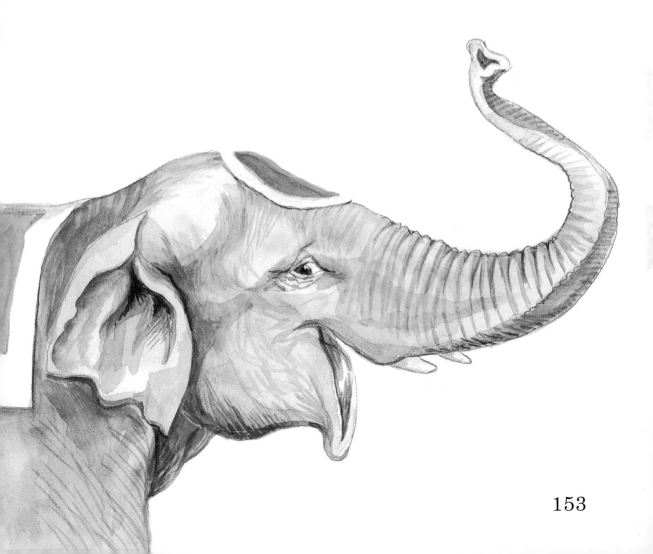

153

154

When you're laughing,
When you're laughing
The sun comes shining thru,

But when you're crying
    You bring on the rain,

So stop your sighing,
Be happy again,

Keep on smiling
'Cause when you're smiling,
The whole world
smiles with you.

Slowly ticks the big clock;

Tick-tock, Tick-tock!

But Cuckoo clock ticks double quick;

Tick-a-tock-a, tick-a-tock-a,

Tick-a-tock-a, tick!

author unknown
picture by Kiyoaki Komoda

160

HOT * YOGA

HOT * YOGA

ENERGIZING, REJUVENATING, HEALING

MARILYN BARNETT

BARRON'S

First edition for the United States and Canada published in 2004
by Barron's Educational Series, Inc.
Reprinted in 2005, 2006, 2007, 2009 and 2010
250 Wireless Boulevard
Hauppauge, NY 11788

All inquiries should be addressed to:
Barron's Educational Series, Inc.
250 Wireless Boulevard
Hauppauge, NY 11788

http://www.barronseduc.com

International Standard Book Number 978-0-7641-2528-7
0-7641-2528-1

Library of Congress Catalog Card Number 2002113755

Conceived and produced by
Elwin Street Limited
144 Liverpool Road
London N1 1LA

www.elwinstreet.com

Editor: Susannah Marriott

Designer: Tracy Timson

Photographer: Mike Prior

Models: Susie Brown and Derek "Agile" Jones

Clothing: Sweaty Betty and Bloch

Disclaimer: The publishers, author, and copyright holder disclaim
any liability for any injury that may result from the use, proper or
improper, of the information contained in this book.

This book is neither endorsed nor affiliated with Bikram Choudhury
or the Yoga College of India.

Printed in Singapore
10 9 8 7 6

CONTENTS

INTRODUCTION

Hatha yoga–the practice of *asana*, or postures–is a physical form of yoga. Essential to practicing the postures is breath control, focus, and relaxation; and many physical and mental benefits accrue as a result of these. On a physical level, as the body's potential for flexibility and strength develops, circulation to the tissues is increased, bringing nourishment to more cells, stimulating the proper functioning of every body system, from the digestion to the nervous system, and increasing energy. The accelerated cellular function resulting from the process releases toxins and waste. As the body begins to function more efficiently, the better we begin to feel. The breath control and concentration each posture demands ensure that we slow down and experience our inherent calmness. All in all, after yoga practice we feel great and suddenly have a new awareness and clarity of thought. We see and respond to life differently.

There are some 80 different asanas or poses in hatha yoga, with thousands of variations. There are also many styles of yoga and schools of thought on how to practice. Hot yoga, which is described in detail on pages 12 to 15, is a practice of asanas in a heated room. One of these hot yoga styles is Bikram Method yoga, for which I am a certified teacher. This book features

my teaching of the Bikram Method style of hot yoga both in a classroom setting and at home. The method of Bikram yoga I teach draws on my many years' experience studying with teachers of other styles of yoga as well as my knowledge of the human body from my medical background. This combination has allowed me to experience incredible breakthroughs in my postures, and I love to share this information with my students. By nature I am an inquisitive person, and I seek solutions to obstacles. I find that the "how to" detail offered in my hot yoga classes makes them special.
I include a detailed section on preparing the mind and body for practice. Additionally, I suggest variations on the traditional Bikram Method postures to make them attainable for those with less flexibility or strength.

Writing this book has been an incredible tool in exploration for me.
I will be forever grateful to the publishers for the opportunity it has given me to go deeper into the understanding of what I love to teach.
I hope you, too, will gain in self-understanding through your hot yoga practice.

New York, May 2003

WHY HOT YOGA?

Yoga is known to restore vitality, heal, and help prevent a range of common chronic ailments. Best of all, it is accessible to everyone: anyone can begin to practice yoga postures, regardless of current levels of strength or degrees of flexibility. The alchemy of hatha yoga is only augmented by practicing yoga postures in a hot room. Add heat to the environment, and along with the sweat, breath, and the development of a foundation, you find the elixir of life within yourself. Heat aids the stretching process while challenging the focus of the mind, enhancing the transformational experience of yoga. When you begin devoting time to yourself through yoga practice, you find the postures and the mindful breathwork that accompanies them bring together your mind, body, and soul, lifting your spirit and giving you a gift of love. Let yoga exercise your heart not with a physical workout alone, but by giving you the energy to reach out with kindness and compassion to raise the spirits of everyone around you.

WHAT IS YOGA?

Yoga is the ancient Indian science of self-discipline. The Sanskrit word *yoga* means union, and yoga practice is a path of self-exploration that unites the mind, body, and spirit, enabling you to become your highest self.

The physical practice of postures and breathing that most people in the West associate with yoga is known as hatha yoga. Other forms of yoga are *karma* yoga, doing good works; *inana* yoga, study and intellectual understanding; and *bhakti* yoga, devotion to the divine. Within hatha yoga one can practice some 80 different postures, with thousands of variations, and many schools and styles of yoga work with various combinations of these asanas.

Patanjali, a great ancient sage and founder of the science of yoga, set out in his *Yoga Sutra* (third century B.C.E.–C.E.) a recipe for attaining the state of yoga, which he defines as the cessation in the fluctuation of the mind. In his eight-fold path of yoga, physical practice of *asana*, body postures, and *pranayama*, breath control, are just two of the eight aspects (see box), cleansing and strengthening the body to enable the remaining aspects, such as concentration and meditation, on the path to self-realization. But comprehending the theory is not enough. To understand yoga, you must practice it–with experience you think, you feel, then you know.

THE EIGHT-FOLD PATH
(eight yogic disciplines)

Yama–self-restraint from violence, lies, stealing, promiscuity, and greed (the code of conduct)

Niyama–observance of cleanliness, contentment, determination, self-study, and surrendering to the highest

Pranayama–controlled breathing

Asana–posture-practice

Pratyahara–withdrawal of the senses (withdrawing from objects of desire, mastery of the senses)

Dharana–concentration (focusing the mind)

Dhyana–meditation (maintaining attentiveness to the object of focus)

Samadhayah–superconsciousness (undistorted truth to nature)

Physical benefits

The physical practice of asana works on the body using contraction, stretching, compression, and release of the soft tissues to create openness and evenness. These actions increase tissue circulation just as the opening of a dam sends rushing waters into smaller waterways. Areas of the body once stagnant and starting to deteriorate are flushed out by this action; they then start to receive nourishment and function fully. The increased number of cells in the body boosts the amount of energy produced while decreasing the workload on the organ systems, allowing them to perform at optimum levels, and balancing hormones and the metabolism.

Mental benefits

Yoga is an effective and efficient way to achieve physiological change, but through this process many psychological changes occur, too. Teachers of different styles of hatha yoga offer different levels of psychological and spiritual insight during class, according to their own experience and the tradition of the style. But common to all styles is the fact that when you employ breath-control and concentration in conjunction with asana, it slows the mind and induces relaxation. Overall, yoga brings a decreased resistance in the flow of energy and thoughts, leaving you free to feel, think, and see from a new perspective. The transformation of your life through yoga is a direct result of this increased awareness of who you are and what you reflect out to the world around you affects what you receive back.

Health benefits

Yoga cleans up and reconditions the pathways of physical and mental circulation and communication, bringing about positive health, hygiene, and an overall sensation of well-being. This combination builds a strong constitution that helps to provide resistance and boosts immunity to disease.

Whatever the degree of physical fitness you start out from, you should adjust the intensity and level of your yoga practice according to your physical limitations, in consultation with your medical advisor and a knowledgeable instructor. For women, most teachers of hatha yoga advise avoiding very strenuous workouts during the first day or so of your menstrual period.

Yoga and pregnancy

During pregnancy, heat should be avoided in the first trimester. Thereafter, consult your obstetrician and a certified yoga teacher; it is thought to be safe to continue with many of the poses to which you are accustomed, but during these special months you should not begin any new yoga practices.

WHAT IS HOT YOGA?

Simply put, hot yoga is yoga performed in a heated room. Performing yoga in the heat is a practice that is becoming ever more celebrated, popularized by two main styles of hatha yoga: *Vinyasa* yoga, a flowing series of postures, and Bikram Method yoga, a set series of static asanas.

In Vinyasa yoga, the movement from the flowing sequences loosens the muscles for action and stimulates circulation. In Bikram Method yoga, the static series of postures are sequenced in a specific order to prepare the body to move deeper as the sequence progresses. The heated environment for both styles acts as a catalyst to enhance the process of relaxing the muscles as well as all of the other benefits received from working up a sweat, including detoxifying the body and strengthening the heart. This book features the Bikram Method, for which I am a certified teacher.

Bikram Choudhury was the pupil of Bishnu Gosh, the founder of the Gosh College of Physical Education in Calcutta. Gosh focused on teaching physical development and mastery of a symmetrically, perfectly developed body using the science of yoga. Within this system, physical and mental strength develop simultaneously through a focus on attention and awakening the energy of willpower. Bikram was to follow in the tradition.

At age 13, Bikram won the National India Yoga Contest, and became an accomplished athlete in cycling, running, and weight lifting. Years later, when Bikram suffered a severe injury to his knee and was told he would never walk again, he returned to his teacher for help.

The healing power of yoga

Within six months under Bishnu Gosh's strict yoga regimen, Bikram underwent a remarkable recovery. With his teacher's encouragement, he began researching health benefits associated with various yoga postures. With this knowledge, he compiled a series of 26 hatha yoga postures which he adapted to address the human body's most common ailments.

The poses are practiced in a set order in a heated room in front of mirrors. After Bikram brought the method to California, it was adopted by the yoga community, spreading across the United States, Europe, and Australia. Two strands of instructors now teach the style or derivations of it. Centers authorized by The Bikram Yoga

College of India offer the method in its traditional form. Other certified instructors, including former Bikram students Baron Baptiste, Jimmy Barkan, and Tony Sanchez, teach their interpretations (to find a class, see page 156). In my hot yoga classes, based on the Bikram Method, I help beginners build a strong physical and mental foundation, something this method of yoga promotes well because of its static nature, repetition, mirrors, and poses that work on strengthening the lower body and spine to maintain an upright posture.

Why the heat?

When your body is cold, you contract, and it becomes difficult to move. As muscles and joints warm, they loosen, decreasing resistance to movement. In a yoga class in a heated environment, there exist external and internal heat. Motion creates heat from the inside out; the heated room provides heat from the outside in, and so you move deeper into a pose with less chance of injury. "Hot" is also a state of mind, suggestive of the intensity of effort and resulting invigoration encouraged by yoga performed in a heated environment.

THE BODY AND HEAT

Many people are drawn to hot yoga because it offers a challenging physical workout for the whole body. With application and practice, athletes, advancing yoga students, and complete beginners alike can benefit from the special qualities heat brings to a workout.

A healthy body maintains a relatively narrow internal temperature range regardless of the environment it inhabits. The nervous system controls body temperature by maintaining the level of the metabolism and regulating heat loss. The largest amount of heat lost from the body results from conduction, or the flow of heat between environments from greater to lesser. By warming the environment, we can stop heat loss through conduction and facilitate the warming of the muscles and the stimulation of the circulation.

Heating the body from the inside is a result of increased metabolic activity. When it is hot, the body acts to avoid overheating and maintain healthy physiological functioning by starting to distribute the heat. It does this by increasing circulation. The heat is transferred from each cell to the fluid between the cells. This is absorbed into circulation and delivered to the surface as sweat. This form of heat loss–evaporation is the body's key way to regulate internal heat during increased heat production.

The benefits of the process

The heat-loss process at work during a hot yoga practice is stimulating and cleansing on many levels. The process of producing sweat to cool the body is a form of passive exercise because it is the reaction of the body to the internal heat accumulation that strengthens it. When the body becomes warm the hypothalamus (located in the brain) activates the body's thermo-regulation systems. The heart rate increases and blood vessels dilate to pump the warmed blood to the surface. This increase in blood flow stimulates the heart to strengthen its contractions which is exercise for the heart muscle itself. As a result, the heart pumps more efficiently thereby lowering diastolic blood pressure. In essence, the heat exposure can be a form of cardiovascular conditioning. Heat also aids in the detoxification process. Increasing blood flow also speeds up the metabolic processes of vital organs, and glands, mobilizing toxins for elimination. Many toxins are encapsulated in fat and stored in the body.

Heat stimulates fat receptors, activating fat stores and facilitating fat loss and releasing these fat-soluble toxins. The skin is the body's largest organ and it plays an important role in detoxifying the body.

Inducing sweat for detoxification purposes is an ancient practice in many traditions. In Ayurveda, *svedhana* (Sanskrit for sweat) is one of the five *panchakarma* or curative therapies. Additional responses of the body to heat include the stimulation of white blood cell production; boosting the immune system; promoting relaxation; and an increase in the speed of healing of connective tissue injuries and peripheral vascular disease symptoms. Overall, the body's response to heat strengthens, detoxifies, and heals, which in turn creates a feeling of well-being.

Balance and efficiency

The combination of internal heat production in the presence of external heat intensifies the experience physically and mentally. Avoiding physical exertion under these conditions requires the discipline of 'balancing the opposites' while 'playing the edge', (see pages 16–17). Try to conserve energy by evenly directing and synchronizing the thought (desire and attention) and breath (energy and space) on the action. Avoid struggling and find the stillness between the thoughts, the breaths, and the postures. The amount and speed of movement,

the nature of the breath, and the intensity of concentration all play a role in heating up a practice. Consider all of the above when setting the temperature of your practice area (see page 33). As your hot yoga practice develops, your ability to move deeper physically and mentally increases your internal heat production and the external heat can then be lowered.

Heat precautions

As humidity levels increase, the apparent temperature also increases, making you feel hotter. It is important to lower the temperature in situations of high humidity because the body's cooling system is ineffective when the sweat cannot be absorbed by the air. Adequate airflow and ventilation to the area can help to push the moisture out. Airflow is also important in the cooling process as it moves the moist air away from the surface and the new air can then absorb more sweat. Caution should be taken to avoid dehydration and overheating which can lead to heat exhaustion. Over time the body acclimatizes and you become heat-conditioned; more blood is pumped to the skin, you start sweating at a lower temperature, and you sweat more water and less salt. Remember that the body needs to acclimatize; if you feel symptoms of overheating, stop to cool off and rehydrate. Kneel on the mat, and drink some water. Never feel pressured to continue whether in class or at home.

DEVELOPING IN MIND AND BODY

Once you make a commitment to change your life through the practice of yoga, you will find yourself developing in mind as well as body as you work through the experience. Physically, you find the strength to be flexible so that you can balance. This is mentally challenging, so you invoke self-discipline, determination, and concentration to keep you going. These in turn increase your patience and give you faith, which strengthens the mind.

Physical achievements

To perform a posture, the body has to move into it. Movement occurs when one muscle shortens and its opposing muscle lengthens. The shortening is caused by contraction, which requires strength; the lengthening is a result of stretching, which requires relaxation. When both occur in equal measure, you acquire the flexibility to be comfortable within a pose. Maintaining this balance allows you to move with grace, some muscles acting as stabilizers, others providing the action. To be in perfect balance, every muscle must be able to contract and/or lengthen equally to maintain the balance of opposites as you perform a movement.

Mental growth

The process of finding physical balance challenges the mind as well as the body. First,

THE PATH TO PROGRESS

- Strength–being strong and relaxed
- Flexibility–becoming comfortable
- Balance–moving gracefully
- Self-discipline–remaining committed to your practice
- Determination–not giving up
- Concentration–attending to your intention and to the details
- Patience–a virtue that, together with all the above, gets you what you want
- Faith–trusting the process and believing in yourself

you need the self-discipline to stay committed to your yoga practice. Second comes the determination that keeps you from giving up when you get frustrated. As you calm down, you begin to concentrate on what you are trying to bring about, and start to observe the tiny accomplishments taking place. These results boost your patience and keep you working toward your goal because you have faith in the process. And when you realize that the process worked because you made it happen by yourself, your willpower and self-esteem get a welcome boost, too.

Personal growth

Let your yoga practice be a personal growth experience. During your practice, be honest with yourself, and accept where you are in the stages of growth as you work continually to improve yourself. Obstacles inevitably present themselves. With each obstacle you encounter, pause and examine it; ask yourself what it is and why it's here right now; figure out how to move forward while in its presence. When you understand something, you can let go of fear and resistance, relying on the process to move you through it. Finally, keep close to your heart the principles of Patanjali's eight-fold path (see page 10), set out so many hundreds of years ago. His *Yoga Sutra* contains three aphorisms that define and describe asana practice. First, keep the pose steady and firm, the mind calm and content.

Second, be aware that perfection occurs when your effort is relaxed during the extension of the mind, body, and awareness. Third, it is at this point that dualities cease to exist. And so, during each posture you work on, focus on being strong, steady, and calm while maintaining an even breath, and focus on the infinite; at this point, the poles of opposites are balanced. Working in this way, you stay detached from results and so move through the process of mental, physical, and personal growth with greater ease.

PLAYING THE EDGE

When working through your personal imbalances, recognize your strengths and weaknesses while you maintain a balance between the two. Learn to play the edge at which comfort meets discomfort, just being there and becoming one with the action. This makes the practice enjoyable and echoes Patanjali's sutras on asana: keep calm, breathe evenly, and meditate on infinity.

HOW THE BODY WORKS

To understand how your body works within yoga poses, you need some knowledge of its structure and mechanical functions. Three systems work together to allow us to move–the skeletal, muscular, and nervous systems. The skeletal system (bones) provides a framework and support. Skeletal muscles attached to bones move the bones, and the nervous system communicates messages to the muscles to move, whether intentional (conscious) or habitual (unconscious).

Bones and muscles

The muscular and skeletal systems work together like a lever device, allowing a heavy load to be moved with less effort than would usually be necessary. A lever system comprises a rigid rod (here, a bone or group of stabilized bones), a fulcrum or pivot point (joint), and effort or force to move the rod (muscular contraction).

Bones attach to each other by ligaments, and muscles cross these joints and are attached to bones by tendons at two or more points. The shortening (contraction) of a muscle moves the bone either toward or away from another bone, depending on the nature of the muscle action. An opposing action moves the bone back to its original position, so when one muscle contracts, its opposing muscle lengthens (stretches).

Depending on the movement, several muscles may be involved, some acting as stabilizers,

others providing the action. To be in perfect balance, every muscle must be able to contract and/or lengthen equally to maintain this balance of opposites as you perform a movement.

oints, ligaments, and tendons

To take a step forward in anatomical awareness, you need to understand the function of the joints (where bone meets bone, see page 21) and in which direction movement is allowed. Bones connect to bones with ligaments; muscles connect to bone with tendons. Both are forms of fibrous connective tissue with a limited ability to stretch and contract. Stretching these tissues, especially the ligaments, results in a lack of stability to the area they support. Therefore, being perfectly aligned is very important in achieving maximum range of motion, as only when you are correctly aligned can the muscles stretch evenly. In general, the

sensation of stretching should feel good; a sharp or one-pointed uncomfortable pulling sensation is usually a sign that your alignment is off and the tendons or ligaments are taking the strain.

Props, such as a pole or broomstick, held against the back of the body during forward bending, for example, help you isolate and experience the correct muscular movement, making you more aware of the sensation of perfect alignment in a pose.

MOVING WITH UNDERSTANDING

Unconscious muscular action–habitual patterns of movement–is the biggest obstacle to overcome in achieving correct positioning within a pose. Over the years, we each develop a unique pattern of movement: it may not be consistent with achieving a full range of motion, and it may be one-sided, creating imbalances in musculature. As we consistently initiate movements with these patterns, so we perpetuate the acquired imbalance. The key to breaking this initiation of movement is awareness.

Staying aware

Bear in mind these basics when beginning a movement. First, know the function of the primary joint involved in the action (see opposite). Second, understand the structural alignment that permits the full range of motion. Third, be aware of the effect other joints and bone alignment have on the outcome (for example, changing foot position before bending the knee alters the stretch in the hip). All this information helps you establish and maintain the best alignment in each pose to produce optimum results. Aligning the bone structure allows the muscles involved in a movement to function fully, whether they are acting as stabilizers or movers. Stabilizing and developing a foundation from the bottom up and center out communicates to the nervous systems that it is safe to move, then the muscles respond without resistance. The process of moving requires less effort when you attend to these musts. With all this to remember, it's clear why you should approach each pose with 100% awareness of where you are and where you wish to go.

GETTING TO KNOW YOUR BODY

Because of long-established patterns of movement, you may not be able to achieve perfect alignment within a posture at first. Aim to maintain the best possible alignment for you, then move to your edge. As the body responds, you will move deeper into the desired position.

JOINT MECHANICS

Spine: 33 vertebral bones divided into five segments. There is very little movement in the individual joints of the spine, but as a whole it provides flexibility to the torso that enables a variety of movements.

7 cervical vertebrae: extension and rotation. The first two vertebrae allow the "yes" and "no" head movement.

12 thoracic vertebrae: flexion and rotation.

5 lumbar vertebrae: extension.

5 sacral vertebrae: fused and attached to the pelvis with very strong ligaments that keep pelvis and sacrum moving as one.

4 coccyx vertebrae: fused; also known as the tailbone; no significant function.

Hip: a ball-and-socket joint, but not as flexible as the shoulder joint; allows for a wide range of movement and is very stable.

Knee: a hinge joint that allows only flexion and extension. The thigh and lower leg must be properly aligned before bending the knee to avoid weakening or injuring this joint.

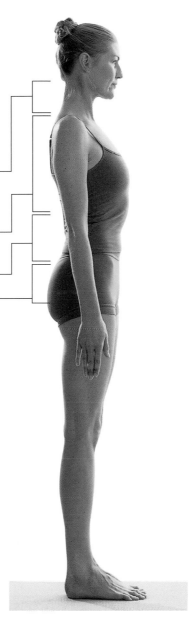

Shoulder: a ball-and-socket joint allowing flexion and extension, adduction and abduction, internal and external rotation, and full rotation. It is very flexible but unstable, so be cautious when working with weight or force, especially if the supportive musculature is out of balance.

Elbow: a hinge joint for flexion and extension, and a pivot joint to allow rotation of the forearm.

Wrist and hand: the multiple bones that make up the hand and wrist provide a variety of movements. These joints are the most flexible part of the body, and their position has an effect on the joints and muscles all the way back to the center of the body. Movement is primarily controlled by muscles in the forearm.

Ankle and foot: as in the wrist and hand, multiple bones here allow considerable movement, and their positioning has a real effect on all the joints and muscles back to the center of the body. Movement is primarily controlled by the lower leg muscles; foot muscles play an important role in stabilizing the leg.

KEY MOVEMENTS

Yoga teaches ways to establish perfect alignment in core areas of the body. Some basic joint movements are also taught in this system to enable students to achieve full flexibility.

ACQUIRING PERFECT ALIGNMENT

Stabilizing the legs (below)
Draw down behind the big toe, pulling in the outer ankle and side of the lower leg up to the knee; push out along the inner thigh. Pull the calves forward and push the thighs back while keeping the back of the knee soft (a micro-bend). Do not push back on the knee when bearing weight on the legs.

Stabilizing the pelvis and spine (left)

Use the points of a diamond shape as an imaginary guide—one at the tip of the pubic bone, one opposite at the navel center, the other two at each side of the hip crest. Stretch these points away from each other evenly, leveling out the space. Hold the space open. After stabilizing the pelvis, work with an imaginary diamond shape in the chest, stretching its points away to open the space. Find the points for the chest in the notch at the top of the sternum, at the navel center, and just below the underarms at both sides of the rib cage. Keep the pelvic and chest diamonds open on a straight line.

Keeping the chest open (right)

Imagine the chest as an open book, its spine in the center. Stretch from the sternum out to the side of the ribs.

BASIC YOGA MOVEMENTS

Forward bending (below)
The hip joint is the pivot for forward bends; the
pelvis pivots over the legs as the body folds in
half. The spine attaches to the pelvis; lengthened
and stabilized, it acts as a lever, stretching the
back of the legs and pelvis as the angle closes
when the two lines come together. For standing
forward bends, keep your weight in the front of
the feet, heels stretching down to protect the
back of the knees. If necessary, bend the knees.

Twisting (above)
Lengthen the spine and rotate the thoracic spine
to bring the shoulder in line with the opposite
hip. Turn the head after completing the twist.

Backward bending (below)

Lengthen the lumbar (lower back) and cervical spine (neck) to open the curvatures in the spine, and arch back the thoracic (upper) spine. Let strength in the back of the body support the backward arc as the front of the body relaxes and opens up over it. Make sure there is no compression in either the lumbar or the cervical curvatures.

Rounding the spine forward (below)
Lengthen the spine to open up the curvatures.
Stretch open the back of the cervical and lumbar
spine, round the thoracic spine, and lift the front
of the body against the spine to support the arc
while the back of the body stretches over it. This
is the reverse of backward bending. Make sure
the stretch to the spine is evenly distributed
along its entire length.

Side bending (right)
When arching the spine to the side, keep the
hips and shoulders squared, ears over shoulders.
Stabilize the pelvis and lengthen the spine,
lifting and twisting through the thoracic spine as
it arcs to one side. Lift along the side to support
the arc; stretch evenly between hip and shoulder.

Sitting-up (below)

To perform a sit-up from lying on your back, inhale your arms overhead. Exhaling, tighten your seat and flex your feet. Keeping the legs and buttocks strong, firm your abdominals and inhale steadily while raising your arms past your ears to shoulder level. At the same time, lift your head and spine up to sitting. Exhale your pelvis over your legs. Inhale and open the spine into the front of the body. Exhale and take the spine forward from the groin up.

TROUBLESHOOTING COMMON PROBLEMS

Uneven use of the body

Repetitive one-sided moves or overuse of one area create an uneven musculature; if you remain unaware of this, the body continues with the pattern, strengthening it.

What you can do: Examine yourself carefully in neutral before beginning a pose. Correct your alignment, finding your center by leveling the body, then set up a good foundation, keeping right and left sides of the spine even. Maintain full awareness as you move, paying attention to the base of your foundation: go down into the foundation before moving steadily up and out. Remember that the pose forever changes as the body develops.

Faulty foot alignment

Correct foot and ankle positioning is vital to establish the alignment that provides maximum range of motion in the joints. Overstretching the outer ankle creates an imbalance in the outer lower and inner upper leg. Repetitive action perpetuates this imbalance and limits flexion and extension of the ankle, knee, and hip joints. When sitting on the heels, the inside edges of the feet should touch, fully extending the foot and lower leg. When the heels drop to the side to avoid this stretch, the outer ankle stretches.

What you can do: If the front of the ankle is really tight, support it with a rolled towel or mat, so your bodyweight does not overstress the joint. Or try this hands and knees maneuver: stretch one leg back, pull the ankle in, and point all five toes evenly away from the front of the knee, heel aligned with the back of the knee. Hold, make a slight internal rotation of the leg, then, bending the knee, bring it down beneath the hip, lower leg and top of the foot resting on the floor. Repeat with the other leg, then sit back on the heels, legs folded comfortably together.

Over-stretching isolated segments of spine

This is an issue in forward bends when the spine remains unstabilized and the top of the body begins to drop below the line of the fold. The problem also occurs in forehead to knee poses where the spine rounds forward.

What you can do: Forward bending is all about hip flexion: the pelvis rotates or pivots forward into the thighs, stretching the back of the thighs and buttocks. The hip joint is the pivot point; the spine is attached to the pelvis and, when stabilized, works with the pelvis like a lever to stretch the muscles required for full hip flexion. Once the spine rounds forward, you lose that stretch; stretching occurs only in the rounding spine. To stretch the spine over the legs, work on pelvic flexion and spinal extension. Beware of trying to pull a rounded back over the legs: this tugs at the spine instead of pulling the pelvis forward into the thighs.
In forehead to knee poses, focus on arching the spine evenly over the femur (thighbone). Lengthen the cervical and lumbar spine prior to flexion to avoid overstretching areas of the spine at which the curvature changes direction.

Compressing the neck and lower back

Comfortable backward bending requires full extension then hyper-extension of the chest and hips: the spine lengthens and arches back, opening the front of the body. Compressing the cervical and lumbar spine prevents full extension, so pressure or pinching here is a warning to correct your position.

Dropping the head back before lengthening the cervical spine and lifting the thoracic spine into the chest strains the neck and may increase cervical compression. The weight of the head pulls the top of the spine down, making it difficult, if not impossible, to lift the thoracic spine. Depending on the pose, it can increase lumbar compression, too.

What you can do: Full backward bending is not needed for the postures in this book, but being aware of its anatomy helps you approach the poses that lead up to it. In the full backbend, the body arches back between hands and feet: the pelvis drops, making the tailbone the highest point of the spine, and the sacrum and thoracic spine lift as the spine continues to lengthen between arms and legs.

To ensure comfort while extending the spine, do not tilt the pelvis forward; this only increases lumbar compression because the sacrum is attached to the pelvis, and to bring the spine up and back without opening the hips causes the lumbar spine to bend back sharply. When dropping the head to look up, or releasing it back during deeper backbends, bring the chin away from the throat, and shoulders away from the ears rather than bending the neck.

Scrunching shoulders

Tightness in the neck and shoulders is common when a rounded back causes the muscles that hold the spine upright to overstretch: the imbalance in the chest and back affects the shoulders and arms. When the arms rise, the shoulders move toward the ears, and stretching is felt in the side of the ribs. Holding the arms up increases the tension and becomes uncomfortable.

What you can do: Open the chest from sternum to sides, ears over shoulders, chin in neutral. Lengthen the arms by the sides, palms in; relax the shoulders down while bringing the forearms toward the sides, and straighten the arms before rotating them away from the body. Inhale, raise the forearms, exhale, relax the shoulders, and lengthen the neck and arms. Continue until the arms are over the shoulders. Bring the forearms in, palms lightly touching.

Try also a full "yes" and "no" movement to flex and extend the cervical spine and boost thoracic and cervical rotation. Open the chest and lengthen the arms as above. Then inhale the chin toward the throat, lifting under the ears and into the notch at the base of the skull. Exhale, relaxing the shoulders while straightening the arms. Inhale the chin to neutral, and exhale, relaxing the shoulders while lengthening the neck under the ears. Repeat, extending into the base of the skull while lifting beneath the chin to stretch the throat. Inhale the chin to neutral, and exhale, relaxing the shoulders while lengthening the neck as before. Inhale, rotating the head over the right shoulder, exhale to center, then repeat to the left.

HOT YOGA AT HOME

When beginning yoga, take classes with a qualified instructor to get familiar with your body and movement patterns while under a watchful eye. Then use the information in this book to increase your understanding of the biomechanics of each posture, applying this knowledge to your practice. Once you feel comfortable and have a basic sense of the postures, set up a home workout space to explore the detail of each pose at your own pace.

The space

Find a quiet place free from distractions with access to heating and a well-positioned mirror. Think about the type of flooring: padded carpet challenges your stability and makes it difficult to balance in one-legged standing poses.

Heating

A radiant space heater provides the best localized heat, since objects near it absorb heat-waves. Air-blowing heaters suffice to heat an area that can be closed off to contain the heat. Heat your space to 100˚F (37.8˚C). Take care when working out in a warm environment, and monitor yourself to avoid overheating.

Mirror view

Full mirror visibility is ideal, but you may need to compromise because of expense and space limitations. The more you can see in a mirror without moving your head, the better for checking your alignment. To view every yoga position would require a mirror as high and wide as you are tall with arms overhead. However, as the poses in this book include only one posture that requires a full-width view, feel free to compromise with a near shoulder-width view in a framed portable mirror. Once you establish the sensual perception of correct alignment, the mirror becomes less important.

Yoga mat

Mats come in various thicknesses; standing and balancing on a thick, spongy mat during hot yoga can be difficult, and sweaty feet slide on a shiny mat. I find a 1/4-inch (6 mm) mat comfortable for all postures; the 1/8-inch (3 mm) mat may not provide enough cushioning for poses on the knees, back, or abdomen unless the floor is carpeted. Some mats have a smooth, shiny surface; others are dull and rough-looking. Rough-textured mats are not easy to find, but are best for sweat yoga. Alternatively, place towels or an absorbent pad on your mat.

During home practice and when taking part in a timed class, keep props close at hand. Move the mat according to the instructions given at the start of each pose to gain the best mirror view for each posture.

Clothing

Besides being comfortable and allowing full range of motion, your clothing must reveal the shape of your body for visual monitoring of alignment. Stretchy, fitted garments are best. If you are uncomfortable in this type of workout wear, choose shorts so that at least your foot to knee alignment is visible. A sports bra is ideal for women; many men choose not to wear a shirt. Most important is to feel comfortable physically and mentally. For class, keep in mind that teachers can't correct what they cannot see.

Towel and washcloth

Keep a towel or two handy to place over your mat for safety and hygiene. Using a towel to absorb moisture keeps your mat cleaner and helps prevent slipping. Place a clean towel at the top of the mat during floor postures as a barrier for your face. Unique to hot yoga, wash-cloths prevent the hand and feet slipping in foot-holding postures. Some people just blot the hands and feet; others hold the cloth between the hand and foot. Do away with it as you develop in the pose and no longer need to grip.

Water

Hydration is essential for peak physical and mental performance. Make sure you are well hydrated before beginning practice, and keep water or an electrolyte drink available to replace fluid lost in sweating.

Hot props

Props help you progress in a pose by providing support or creating a physical environment that allows only the correct action for developing the posture. Foam blocks and folded or rolled blankets, towels, or even washcloths make good support props, raising your foundation to meet your inflexibility. They can be placed, for example, in front of the ankles when kneeling, behind the head when lying supine, or used to extend the arms in standing forward bends, taking pressure off the inflexible area and allowing the body to maintain alignment. Strength and flexibility develop evenly once the body is fully grounded into such a foundation. Select your prop according to your level of inflexibility or misalignment; as you develop, decrease the height of the prop, and eventually eliminate it.

Props are also a great way to isolate movement when learning how to approach a posture; a wall, door, pole, or blocks offer something to stabilize against, allowing you to move in the direction of the posture using contraction and relaxation. You might, for example, stand against

Foam blocks make good support tools. Here, they allow the body to remain aligned in the pose. A rolled washcloth takes pressure off the ankles.

a wall to establish proper front-to-back alignment, or try forward bending with a pole held against your back. To reinforce standing upright, try standing facing the narrow edge of an open door with feet on either side of the door beneath the hips. Bring the spine forward to hold the front of the body up against the door edge. Using props in this way is best confined to self-exploration or private lessons.

PREPARING FOR PRACTICE

Yoga practice offers valuable time to spend with yourself that enhances your physical, mental, and spiritual qualities. Being prepared makes the journey that much more enjoyable and effective. Plan ahead by setting aside adequate time and preparing yourself physically and mentally; you will then be able to focus fully on your intentions when it is time to begin.

PREPRACTICE RITUALS

- Be hydrated: drink plenty of water throughout the day. Excessive amounts of liquid just before class may not be comfortable and you may need to disrupt your practice to relieve yourself.

- Don't eat a heavy meal within two hours of practice: the stomach should be empty for yoga. If you do need to eat, choose easily digestible food.

- Take a hot bath if you feel stiff or need relaxing.

- Center yourself: take a few moments to be still and feel your breath, allowing yourself just to be.

- Mentally dedicate your practice to yourself.

When you start your practice, work through every pose efficiently, playing each edge as if you will be in the pose forever. In this way, yoga becomes a meditation in motion and you find yourself contemplating the infinite. This gradual process is effective in helping you develop each movement from the bottom up and the inside out; and so you build a solid pose.

Working with the breath

Use your breath to help you work through the postures, mindfully synchronizing it with the thought, feeling, and action of the move. Breathe in through the nose and out through the mouth, using the throat to control the volume, and mentally directing the flow of air through the body. With each inhalation, draw strength in from your foundation and take space to restricted areas. As you exhale, stabilize your foundation and relax tension around newly created space, moving deeper in the direction of the desired pose.

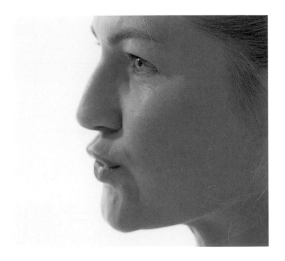

Setting up for breathing

Softly close your lips and use your throat to monitor the flow of breath, drawing it in slowly and evenly, and filling the lungs fully from bottom to top. Then open your mouth and let the breath out with the same control, emptying the lungs completely. The breath is audible: when you inhale it is a high-pitched "HUMMMMM;" the exhalation sounds like a low-pitched "HAAAAA." Treat the inhalation and exhalation as separate actions, completing each one before beginning the next. Make the transition between them smooth so that you don't begin with a quick rush of air. This would cause the top portion only of the lungs to fill or empty, making it difficult to complete the action.

If you have problems controlling the flow of breath, work on evenness, making sure you don't gasp in or expel out too much air at once. In the first pose (pages 40–43), work up to a full six-second intake and expelling of breath, keeping it even from the very beginning to the end in each direction. As the capacity of your lungs increases, resistance decreases and you will be able to move more air during the 6 seconds.

TADASANA

To begin your yoga practice and between each standing posture you adopt a basic standing pose known as Tadasana or Samasthiti. The feet stand parallel to each other (as shown opposite) and all the joints are aligned so that the body remains in line from ears to ankles through the center of the joints. The eyes, shoulders, and hips stay level.

Setting up for Tadasana

Place your feet parallel to each other: visualize a line from the base of each second toe to the center of the ankle on each foot and place them parallel. Bring the knuckles of the big toes to touch and place your heels directly behind your toes. Lift your toes, stretch the ball of the foot wide, and press down into the floor. Relax the toes lightly on the floor while keeping your weight evenly distributed between the sides of the heels and the balls of the feet, which anchor to the floor.

Take your thighs back so the hips are directly over the heels, knees centered between hip and ankle; there should be a softness or microbend behind the knee.

Square up your pelvis and shoulders (see stabilizing the pelvis and spine, page 23), and bring your ears over your shoulders, chin parallel to the ground.

With arms at your sides, palms facing in, hold your chest open and draw the elbows toward the body. Stretch your palms open, then relax the arms and hands. Soften your eyes and gaze straight ahead. If necessary, keep your toes up to stabilize the upright alignment. If having the knuckles of the big toes touching feels unstable or uncomfortable because the knees or thighs are too close, separate the feet slightly.

RELAXATION IN SAVASANA

Dead Body Pose, Savasana, is the finishing touch to your practice and one of the most important poses to follow any yoga routine. You will find instructions for final Savasana in a class setting on pages 152-155. At home, props such as pillows, blocks, or folded blankets can help you more readily to find the state of deep relaxation brought about by Savasana. Beginners and less flexible students especially benefit from this approach.

Savasana between postures

Savasana forms the transition between the standing and floor postures. Once you have finished Tree Pose (see pages 88-91) and have taken two breaths in Tadasana, lie back on your mat for two minutes of quick relaxation. Return to this neutral place again after each floor pose. Between the spine-strengthening postures, use a version of the pose lying on your front during the brief transition between the poses.

Using props in Savasana

Choose a light blanket or shawl to protect you from drafts; use blankets or towels as suggested:

Supporting the head

- Use a rolled blanket or towel to support the curve in your neck.
- Add support to either side of your head with rolled towels or pillows for a little extra treat.
- Cover your eyes with a soft cloth or eye pillow to aid withdrawal from the outside world.

Supporting the arms

- Place a folded towel or thin pillow beneath your forearms to support your wrists and hands and provide elevation to ease returning circulation.
- Fold a towel to make a support at least as wide as your chest and approximately 4-6 inches (10-15 cm) in length. Place it between your underarms and shoulder blades to create a slight upper-back bend that gives the chest a gentle stretch and promotes opening in the heart center.

Supporting the legs

- Place a folded blanket or bolster beneath your knees to support them if, when you fully extend your legs, your pelvis tilts out of neutral. This

removes pressure from the lower back and is promotes complete relaxation.

- Draw the soles of the feet together and up, then place supports beneath the outside of the knees and legs as they relax (shown above).

Letting go

Students of yoga use a variety of visualization and breathwork techniques to help let go of extraneous thoughts as well as tension in the body during this final relaxation. Experiment with the suggestions here:

Using the breath

Inhale slowly from fingertips to shoulders. Roll the breath around the shoulder joints, and slowly exhale through the elbows, past the wrists and hands, and out through your fingers. Inhale slowly into your navel, draw the breath up the spine to the back of your head, and slowly exhale through your face, throat, chest, and out through your belly. Inhale slowly through the tips of your toes, taking the breath up your legs into your hips. Gently squeeze the buttocks, release, and exhale down the legs past the knees, ankles, feet, and out through your toes. Inhale again, taking the breath from the soles up through your body to your crown. Pause, and exhale very slowly through the entire body, releasing all fear, worry, and tension.

Giving thanks and just being

Adopting an attitude of gratitude, breathe in and allow thanksgiving to fill you. Breathe out and feel love surrounding you. Count your blessings with each breath.

Inhale a slow, full, deep breath. Exhale a long, releasing breath and allow yourself simply to be. Practice being more and doing less.

THE POSES

Within this chapter you will find instructions for poses practiced in a Bikram Method hot yoga class. We start with standing poses (overleaf), and then move onto poses practiced lying or kneeling on the floor. Correctly positioning and aligning the body within each pose is of key importance, since only in this way are you able to bring about the desired response of body and mind to a particular posture. Once you begin to feel the difference between a correct and incorrect posture, you quickly become able to reposition yourself. Treat the instructions for each pose in the pages that follow, with their great detail and intense scrutiny of positioning, as virtual teachers, consulting the hot tips to check on your alignment and movement within each stage of an asana, and to troubleshoot common problems. Be patient with yourself; this book offers a great deal of information, and assimilating it into your practice takes time. Each body is unique, and every one of us will work through many stages of development in a pose. Where necessary, I suggest alternative ways to approach a posture as you develop the balance between strength and flexibility required to perform the pose in the tradition of the style. Some of the alternatives are modifications that isolate the movement so that you use the right muscle groups. This allows you to connect with the sensation, providing a physical as well as a mental understanding of the intention behind each pose. Whatever your starting point, enjoy your practice.

STANDING DEEP BREATHING

PRANAYAMA

Warm up with a breathing exercise (the Sanskrit word *prana* means breath or life-force) that begins to warm the body, open the airways, and stimulate the lungs. As the air moves deeply in and out of the lungs, their capacity is increased. When performed correctly, the head and arm movements that accompany the breath lengthen, relax, and strengthen muscles in the shoulders, arms, neck, chest, and upper back while empowering the stabilizing muscles of the shoulder joints. Mentally, slow and controlled breathing calms the mind and connects you with your body as you actually begin to feel yourself breathe. Beginners may find it easier to practice the breath technique on page 34 separately before putting it together with the body movements. Throughout, work on maintaining even control of the flow of breath: try not to gasp in or expel out too much air at once.

STARTING POSITION: *top of the mat toward the mirror; standing at the center of the mat facing the mirror.*

SETTING UP From Tadasana, basic standing pose (see pages 34-35), interlace your fingers to the webbing and place your knuckles under your chin. Keep your chin down, neck in a neutral position. Point your elbows to the floor, separated to make a straight line from second knuckle to elbow. Straighten your wrists, relax your shoulders, and open your chest. Gaze straight ahead. The chin and knuckles stay connected through all four movements. Try to keep your body stable and still; only your arms and head move. Use the breath technique on page 34.

1 Arms only

Keeping your chin down, start separating your elbows and circle your arms up and in toward your ears. Keep your wrists straight, shoulders relaxed, and neck long. Draw your arms down into the shoulder joints as they circle upward, raising them as high as you can without lifting shoulders to ears. Feel the movement in your arms, shoulders, and upper back, rather than as a lifting and stretching from the middle of the torso. Sense a nice opening and stretching of the palms as the elbows move toward your head.

Hot tips Don't let the shoulders rise when you bring the arms up. Lengthen the muscles around the neck, shoulders, and arms to bring the arms up closer to the ears. Initiate arm movements with the forearm bone.

2 Head only

Keeping your neck neutral and stable, lift your chin away from your throat (pivot the head up as if beginning the "yes" head movement) to stretch the throat. Keep your knuckles and chin connected and your elbows up. Take your gaze upward. Be careful not to crunch the back of the neck.

3 Arms only

Keeping the elbows up, bring your forearms toward each other without bending your wrists or moving your torso. Try to keep your forearms parallel with the ceiling, your body parallel with the mirror. Don't let the front of the body collapse to touch elbows.

4 Head only

Bring your chin back toward your throat, elbows pointing down in the starting position. After each set of movements, return your arms to your sides, bring your chin into your throat, and relax your head and shoulders down to the basic standing pose. Begin setting up again and work up to 10 cycles, ending with the fourth movement.

WORKING THE POSE When putting all the movements together, inhale during step 1, pause the breath on the transition, then complete the second step. Exhale during step 3, pause during the transition, and again before completing the final step. As you become more comfortable at putting it all together and are able to maintain an awareness of the breath and movements simultaneously, make the sequence more continuous by beginning the exhalation on the second move, completing it with the third move, beginning the inhalation on the fourth move, and completing it with the first move. It goes like this—inhale, arms circle upward; exhale, chin up and arms circle around; inhale, chin down and arms circle. Be careful not to cheat yourself of the entire range of motion you experience when completing each movement fully.

HALF-MOON POSE WITH HANDS-TO-FEET POSE

ARDHA CHANDRASANA & PADAHASTASANA

You take on the form of a crescent moon (*ardha* means half, *chandra* moon) in this second standing pose in the series, which awakens and warms up the spine. There are four parts to the pose: by following side bends to the right and left with backward and forward bending, you strengthen and lengthen all four sides of the spine, and stretch your extremities, too. In the hands-to-feet forward bend, you gradually progress into a deep forward bend that stretches the lower spine and allows gravity to elongate the rest of the spine. It also provides a good stretch for every part of the back of the legs.

STARTING POSITION: *standing at the center of the mat facing the mirror.*

SETTING UP From Tadasana, inhale and raise your arms slowly overhead. Interlace your fingers and release the fourth fingers like a steeple. Exhale, relaxing the shoulders. Draw your elbows in, straightening the wrists and bringing your palms flat together. Do not grip the palms; gently move the forearm bones in while relaxing the shoulders. The wrists and elbows begin to straighten, the chest opens, and the upper back muscles activate to stabilize the shoulder joints and hold the chest open. Aim to stand erect, arms over-head aligned with the ears, spine in a neutral position through all four parts of the pose.

Right side bend

Stabilize your legs and pelvis, then lift the spine vertebra by vertebra out of the pelvis. When you get to the thorax (ribcage area), continue to lift, slightly rotating the right side forward, left side back so the shoulders stay square with the pelvis, the chest open. Relax the shoulders away from the ears, and draw your forearms in, straightening wrist and elbow joints. From the front you resemble a crescent moon, the spine forming the arch between straight legs and arms. Feel your weight evenly distributed in the four corners of your feet. From the side, everything aligns: if standing in front of a wall, legs, hips, both shoulders, head, and arms would touch it. Work with the breath for 1 minute–about 6 breath cycles. Inhale to come up, and exhale. Pause in the center. On the next inhalation begin setting up to bend left.

Hot tips Shoulders scrunching, chest collapsing, or back arching? Set up again, then raise the arms without lifting the shoulders. Stretch up and over a few times. Return to center and check your alignment.

2 Left side bend

Reverse the directions for step 1 to work with the left side. Let the left side of your body support your posture while the right side relaxes and lengthens. Inhale, stabilize your legs, draw strength into the left side of the spine, and move it toward the center. Draw your forearms in, maintain the lift in the center of your torso, and keep your shoulders down. Exhaling, release and lengthen between ankles and hips, hips and shoulders, and shoulders and wrists. Simultaneously stretch the right side of your body from hands to feet while strengthening the muscles that stabilize the left side of your spine. Work with your breath for 1 minute, drawing in strength and space to appropriate areas when inhaling; stabilizing and relaxing into the stretch on the exhalation. Come up on an inhalation, and exhale at the center. On the next inhalation, begin to set up for bending backward.

✳ Hot tips Hinging from the waist or hips when folding to the side? Work on creating alignment on all four sides of the body: start from the inner ankles and sense the line up through the perineum, navel center, heart center, throat center, crown of the head, and along to the inside of the wrists and palms.

3 Backward bend

Draw the calves forward and down, thighs back and up, stabilizing the pelvis and legs (weight in heels). Release the tailbone down and spine up. Relax chin to throat, taking the arms back (head between). Lift the chest with the spine. Don't move the thighs forward: stack leg and hip joints. Making a line from fingertips to lower shoulder blades, inhale, tailbone to heels, stabilize, and open the chest. Exhale chin to throat, head and arms back. Work for 1 minute.

Forward bend

4 Stabilize the legs (take the calves forward, thighs back, lower legs inward, upper legs out). Begin to rotate the pelvis forward, and, maintaining a straight line from fingertips to tailbone (chest up, as if folding in half from the top of the thighs), take your hands to the floor. Let your head hang, shaking "yes" and "no" to release tension. Warm up by walking out the legs–bend one knee at a time and stretch up to the hip of the straight leg. For a different stretch, lift the heel of the bent knee, and bend and straighten both knees together a few times. Then, with bent knees open, flatten out the diamond in the front of the pelvis (pubis to navel, hipbone to hip-bone) and place it on your thighs. There should be no space between pelvis and thighs. Reach around and place your fingers under your heels, cupping the heels, forearms on the back of the calves, elbows pointing upward. Feel the weight in the balls of your feet, heels reaching into your palms. Let the rest of the torso relax over your legs and your head hang. Work with your breath for 1 minute.

Hot tips Can't turn the pelvis because of tightness in the back of the legs? Begin to bend the knees and allow the body to fold in behind. At the groin, bring the front of the hipbones on to the thighs, lower ribs to thighs, chest to knees, hands to the floor.

WORKING THE POSE Connect your ankle bones, outside to inside; inhale; draw your lower legs in, upper legs apart. Exhaling, move your calves forward, thighs back. Keep the pelvis gently pressing flat on the front of the thighs and relax the torso, letting gravity lengthen the spine. Keep your forearms on the back of the calves, back of the lower legs stretching into your palms. Hold the elbows up, shoulders away from ears, crown of the head moving toward your feet. The back of the thighs stretch up to the sitting bones.

Hot tips Can't keep the pelvis on the thighs? Don't continue bending forward. Lifting the diamond shape of the pelvis away from the thighs moves the stretch from the back of the legs, and only an isolated, weak, portion of spine stretches. Continuing to bend forward only increases the flexibility and emphasizes weakness See the tips on forward bending on page 24.
If you are using the body unevenly, see page 28. Try also practicing the pose with feet slightly apart for better stability.

COMING OUT Inhale and lift your chest, creating a line from fingertips to tailbone to stabilize the torso, then lift your hipbones away from your thighs. Bring your body up in one piece from the hip joint (rotating the pelvis back up). In the beginning, you may need to bend your knees when lifting the chest to create a straight energy line from fingertips to tailbone. Then lift your body away from your legs and straighten your legs on the way up. Exhale and take your arms down to your sides.

AWKWARD POSE

UTKATASANA

There are three postures within the third pose of the standing series, which warm up the lower body and the mind. Physically, these stretches work primarily on the legs, strengthening all the muscles here as well as the ankle and knee joints. They also improve core stabilization by toning the abdominals, upper back, and the arms, especially the triceps. As the name suggests–*utkata* signifies powerful or mighty–the movements as well as being awkward to master, test your focus and concentration as you try to maintain complete steadiness of mind and body.

STARTING POSITION: *standing at the center of the mat facing the mirror.*

SETTING UP From Tadasana, separate your feet hip-width apart. Use your front hip-bones as a guide and center your ankles beneath them. Make sure your feet are planted directly beneath your hips so your legs and feet are aligned parallel with each other from the top of the thigh to the ankle to the base of the second toe. Use the midline of your legs, rather than the edges, as your guide. Keep your toes relaxed, resting on the floor. Inhale and raise your arms to shoulder-height. Draw your forearms in to align the arms, straight from the middle finger to the center of the upper arm, and parallel with each other and the floor. Exhale and relax your shoulders. Keep your arms in this position through all three postures. Ensure that your ears are over your shoulders and your chin is parallel to the floor. Keep your chest and abdomen open wide and long, your stomach in and up, your shoulder blades in and down, and let the shoulders relax. Keep your gaze straight ahead and your breath smooth and even.

Hot tips Look at your feet. Too close together or too wide apart and the ankle and hip joints won't align, increasing instability.

Can't hold the arms up without tensing neck, shoulders, and arms? Inhale, drawing the forearms in. Exhale, hold them up (as if heavy), and relax shoulders away from ears. This engages stabilizing shoulder muscles.

1 Fold forward

Folding from the hips, take your body forward and down, raising arms parallel to the floor in an upside-down "L." Lift all ten toes, press down beneath the big toe, then stretch across to the outer edge of the feet, both sides of the heels on the floor. Keep all four corners of the feet evenly anchored. With shins back, knees as wide as feet, upper thighbones in, begin folding at the knees; try to bring the thighs parallel to the floor. Lift the sitting bones to support you. Holding, lift the front hipbones from the thighs, body up as much as possible, as if sitting in a chair. Keep the chin parallel, gaze forward, breath steady. Hold for 10 seconds; come to standing slowly.

2 Lower the body

Keeping your toes relaxed and flat to the floor, shift your weight forward and begin to lift your heels directly behind your ankles as high as you can. Now bend at the knees and lower your body as if sliding down a wall. Ideally, ears, shoulders, hips, and ankles look in line from the side. Come down 8-10 inches (20-25 cm): keep the front of your torso open and back to remain upright and aligned. As you hold your torso steady, keep lifting your heels, trying to bring your feet perpendicular to the floor. Again, keep your chin parallel to the floor, gaze forward, breath smooth and steady. Hold for 10 seconds before slowly coming back to standing.

Hot tips Knees veer in or out of center? Go back to the setting-up instructions to check your alignment and joint movement. When feet aren't evenly grounded and the ankle joints are not stabilized, weight rolls to the inside or outside of the feet. As your flexibility and strength balance out from hips to toes, you'll find it easier to hold everything in place.

3 Touch knees

Lift your heels and bend your knees slightly, keeping your body upright. Turn your legs inward, bringing your knees to touch, heels and sitting bones out. Keep your knees glued together. Again, as if sliding down a wall, lower your hips, letting your knees come down and forward, and trying to descend until your thighs are parallel with the floor. Keep your chin parallel to the floor, your gaze forward, your breath smooth and steady. Hold for 10 seconds.

Hot tips Torso leaning forward? This throws off your center of gravity. Keep your side-view alignment the same as in step 2: ears, shoulders, hips, and ankles all visibly in line.

COMING OUT Ascend slowly in the same way that you went down. Bring your feet back together and take your arms down to your sides.

EAGLE POSE

GARUDASANA

This is the last pose in the warm-up phase of the standing series, named for *garuda*, the eagle. The extremities undergo a twisted-rope type maneuver as you balance in a seated position. The compression and release action of this pose stimulates the 12 major joints in the body–the ankles, knees, hips, shoulders, elbows, and wrists–as well as the pelvic organs. It is also the first pose in which you start to explore balancing on one leg. After finishing this pose you are invited to take a quick water break before starting to work on the balancing standing postures.

STARTING POSITION: *standing at the center of the mat facing the mirror.*

SETTING UP From Tadasana, inhale, raising your arms over your head while relaxing your shoulders away from your ears. Exhaling, gently swing your arms down and around the front of your body, crossing your right arm under your left at shoulder level. Bend your elbows and cross your wrists, palms facing upward. Now bring your palms together in prayer position and cross thumbs.

Hot tips Overrounding and stretching the back when wrapping the arms? This closes the chest and abdominal cavity. Make sure you keep space at the front of the body to take the stretch to areas that are commonly neglected.

1 Arm position

Inhale width and length into the chest cavity, then, as you exhale, retain the space in your chest, draw your abdomen in and up, release your shoulders away from your ears, and take your forearms and hands away from your face, directly above the elbows. Keep your head and neck in a neutral position.

Hot tips As you inhale, lengthen and widen the front of the body by opening the diamond points of the chest and pelvis (see page 23).

2 Fold forward

Inhale again, maintaining the upper body setup. Exhaling, fold forward from the hips, torso parallel to the floor. Inhale space into tight areas, then exhale and fold at the knees, taking the thighs parallel to the floor while keeping your chest open, spine neutral. Inhaling, rotate your pelvis away from your thighs to bring the torso up. Exhale and stabilize as you lift the right heel, toes on the floor, shifting weight off the right leg. Counter-balance the right hip off the left shoulder.

3 Leg position

Inhale and take your right thigh above your left thigh, allowing the right foot to hang below the right knee. Exhale and cross the legs, making an "X" with your thighs, then compress the thighs into each other in a seated position. Inhale, drawing your right knee back to move the hip back, and exhale, leveling the hips and squaring up your torso. Working with the breath, bring your lower legs toward each other and reach the right foot around the left calf, hooking your big toe around the inner part of your left ankle. Continue working to close any gaps in your intertwined extremities while remaining seated upright with chest and abdomen open. Hold for 10 seconds.

COMING OUT At the end of an exhalation, slowly release your twisted arms and legs and, as you begin inhaling, stand up, bringing your arms overhead and exhaling them down and around to repeat the pose on the other side. This time, cross your left arm beneath your right arm, your left leg over your right leg. After holding on this side, exit the pose and immediately reenter on the right side to start a second set on both sides. Once you have released the left side for the second time, return to Tadasana, practicing stillness for two breaths.

STANDING HEAD-TO-KNEE POSE

DANDAYAMANA-
JANUSHIRASANA

The following three standing poses introduce balancing on one leg–*danda* means a stick or staff. In all three, let your primary focus in the beginning be on keeping your standing leg straight and stable while you progress through the movements. Imagine you have no knee, your leg resembling a post from heel to hip. This first pose is a forward bend. Your long-term goal is to be able to stand on one leg and extend the other leg parallel to the floor with foot flexed and fingers interlaced behind it, elbows dropped below the calf and spine rounded over the extended leg, forehead touching the knee. This sounds like a phenomenal feat, and the finished pose is very impressive. However, your first goal is to develop increment by increment, and to strike a balance between strength and flexibility. It is more important to perfect the stages of development than to achieve the big picture.

STARTING POSITION: *standing at the center of the mat facing the mirror.*

forward, thigh back, lower leg in, upper leg out. These opposing actions stabilize the knee joint and keep it from bending. As you do this, pick up the right thigh to parallel. Keep your standing leg stable and torso square as you move the right leg.

1 Leg extension

Once you have established steadiness, pivot forward from the hips, keeping your torso extended over your right thigh until your thigh is parallel with the floor. Keep your abdomen in and upper body up to prevent your center of gravity from shifting forward. Place your interlaced hands beneath the arch of your right foot and immediately kick your heel forward, in line with the hip. Allow your arms to extend fully. Keep your chest open and up, away from the extended leg. Work on this stage until you can fully extend your right leg with foot flexed. Level your hips and square up your body.

Hot tips Rounding your spine over the extended leg? Extending the heel above or below the hip joint? Torso not staying square? Don't rush ahead without acknowledging the details: you won't develop the foundations necessary for support, and without support you can't adequately release inflexibility. The resistance between strength and flexibility simply exhausts your energy.

SETTING UP Standing with feet parallel, hip-width apart, lift your right heel and lightly rest the ball of your foot directly under your right hip, knee softly bent. Level out your hip line and square your shoulders. Aim to keep the diamond points of the chest and pelvis open wide (see page 23). Keep your shoulders relaxed, ears over your shoulders, chin parallel, and eyes focused straight ahead. Begin to stabilize your left leg. Keeping ankle, knee, and hip aligned, direct your muscular energy as follows: calf

2 Lower the torso

Slowly fold in at the elbows, lowering your torso over the extended leg until your elbows are just below your calf. Once again, adjust any misalignment, then very slowly tuck your chin into your throat, pull back through your lower abdomen and, lifting up from the center, place your forehead on your knee, as shown on page 60. Hold and breathe, aware that this pose is one minute long from beginning to end. As you develop the strength and flexibility required for steady movement, you will gain time to fine-tune this stage.

Hot tips Challenge yourself without making too many compromises, and whenever you lose your stability, back up, regain what you lost, and begin again to work with your breath to progress steadily through the process. When using the breath, inhale slowly, drawing in strength and space to areas that need them. As you exhale, stabilize and release into needy areas.

COMING OUT Release the pose with the same awareness you came into it, and return to Tadasana. Take a breath and begin setting up to work on the left side. After finishing this side, take two full breaths in Tadasana and begin a second set. This is only 30 seconds long: muscle memory allows the body to progress a little quicker to the stage you achieved in the first set.

STANDING BOW PULLING POSE

DANDAYAMANA-
DHANURASANA

The next challenge in your pursuit of standing-strength and balance is a backward bend–*dhanura* refers to the archer's bow that your spine begins to resemble in the ideal pose. Work toward this ultimate goal by standing and balancing on one leg while holding the opposite foot behind you, arching and then twisting the upper back while kicking your leg up to a standing split. As in the previous pose, progress is best developed by breaking down the posture into stages: only by doing this will you be able to work out and eventually resolve your unique personal combination of imbalances.

STARTING POSITION: *standing at the center of the mat facing the mirror.*

SETTING UP From Tadasana, release your bodyweight from your right leg while establishing the foundation in your left leg, then square up and level the torso just as you did when setting up the previous pose (see page 62).

Hot tips When you grab your foot, ensure that your shoulder does not rotate in toward your chest, closing it. Make sure, too, not to grab the outside of the foot. Try not to lift the shoulder and overextend the side of the body when holding the arm overhead. Progress to the next stage only when you feel happy with step 1.

Bend the leg

Rotate your right arm so the palm and inner elbow face out. Without tilting your pelvis forward, extend your right leg behind, press the ball of the foot into the floor, and straighten your leg (to pre-stretch the thigh and groin). Now draw your right heel to your buttock, pull your arm behind you without changing position, and cradle the arch side of your foot in your palm (thumb toward the toes, inner elbow facing out). Keep your hip-bones up, tailbone down as you bring your thighs together, knees in line. Take your left arm back and circle it overhead, palm forward. Realign yourself, squaring your torso (equalize the length between underarm and hip on both sides, shoulders down and level, hips level) and stabilizing your standing leg.

2 Pivot forward

Slowly pivot from the hips, bringing your torso parallel to the floor. Kick your right heel away from your buttock as you begin to arch the upper back. Let the torso hang as you kick away just enough to keep yourself from falling forward. Keeping the left leg stable, left shoulder in line with the hip, relax your right hip down until even with the left hip. Release your left shoulder from your ear while lengthening your right side from hip to underarm to square the body.

WORKING THE POSE Work on developing evenness in both sides of the body, continuing to open the chest by bending the upper back, and continuing to stretch the right groin by kicking the leg back into your hand and straight up. Keep your hips stabilized on top of your standing leg, and stretch your rib cage away from your hips. Bend your upper back backward, let your extended leg pull your arm back to open the chest, and feel your extended arm lengthen and pull back into the shoulder, keeping both shoulders in line. Make sure your right and left joints stay aligned. Maintain enough tension between the kick back into your hand and the body movement down (chest up) to prevent yourself from falling forward.

Hot tips Joints of the standing leg not aligned? Move your thigh forward, bringing hip and ankle joints in line, then straighten the leg. If your hips are not level, draw the standing leg in and up, then relax your opposite hip down, keeping the torso square. If the shoulder of your front arm moves forward, causing the body to shift off center, draw the arm back to move the shoulder back, and stretch into the opposite armpit to equalize the length of your sides, then align yourself to find your center. Don't move to the next stage until you feel confident here.

3 Spinal twist

Maintaining the integrity of the pose you achieved in step 1, begin to twist the chest while continuing to kick up into the standing splits. Your arms, shoulders, and extended leg eventually align in the center. Let your hand slide to the ankle as your leg goes up. The legs rotate inward as they split. Practice for 1 minute on the first set.

WORKING THE POSE Use your breath to breathe your way to your edges and begin to play at the edge as you continue to maintain integrity and work on your weaknesses. Once you have reached this stage, you might like to start the pose with feet slightly pigeon-toed and legs slightly rotated.

COMING OUT Exit the pose with awareness, reversing the steps you used to enter the pose, and return to Tadasana. Work on the left side, then repeat on both sides, this time holding for 30 seconds.

BALANCING STICK

TULADANDASANA

Often referred to as putting the body into a "T" formation, this is the final standing strength-building pose. You try to hold the body in a stable neutral position parallel with the floor while balancing on one leg. There is nothing to kick or pull against in this balancing position; it is all about stabilization. Although the pose is held for only 10 seconds, it has a noticeable effect on the heart. When you bring the arms overhead and then take the body and extended leg parallel to the floor, there is a sudden increase in the amount of blood returning to the heart, causing it to contract harder in order to pump blood back out to the body. The heart is a muscle and this action strengthens it–in this posture you exercise your heart while developing grace.

STARTING POSITION: *standing at the back of the mat facing the mirror.*

SETTING UP Make sure you have enough room in front to step forward and bend forward with arms overhead. From Tadasana, take your arms overhead on an inhalation and interlace your fingers, releasing your index fingers like a steeple. Exhale and draw your forearms together, straightening your elbows and wrists, palms lightly touching. Release your arms down into the shoulder sockets, and relax your shoulders away from your ears (see setting up for Half-Moon Pose with Hands-to-Feet Pose, page 46).

Hot tips Move back your front thighs, back ribs, back of the head, and arms to align the side-view center of your body. Feel your front-view center aligned through your inner legs, pubis, navel, sternum, center of the chin, nose, and inner wrists through your palms.

1 Lift the leg

Inhale and step forward with your right foot, coming to stand with all the leg joints aligned. Exhale, tilting your pelvis forward and aligning head and body with your left leg. Inhale, draw energy into the standing leg, and rotate the other leg inward while pressing through the width of the ball of the foot. Exhale and stabilize. Inhale, opening the front of the body to square the torso, and lift your extended leg slightly up from the floor while stabilizing the entire body. As you exhale, pivot forward with control from the hips, maintaining joint alignment and stability, to bring your body and extended leg parallel with the floor, as shown on page 70. Keep your chest down and arms up, head between the arms. At the same time rotate the extended leg inward as you hold it level with the hip. Work at your edge for 10 seconds. As you inhale, reach down through the foot of your standing leg and draw energy up the leg into the hip for support. As you exhale, stretch across to the opposite hip and level the hips while stretching the ribs away.

Hot tips Don't let the chest collapse and spine round forward: this looks more like an umbrella than a "T." Pivot in a straight line from the hip joint. Be aware of side-bending when pivoting forward: pay attention to aligning your right and left sides and move slowly, backing up and making corrections before continuing.

COMING OUT On an inhalation, pivot back up until your extended leg touches the ground. Step back with your standing leg and bring your arms down to your sides. Take two full breaths and then begin to work on the left side. Repeat a second set on both sides.

STANDING SEPARATE LEG STRETCHING POSE

DANDAYAMANA-
BIBHAKTAPADA-
PASCHIMOTTHANASANA

The next three standing poses are practiced with legs separated, and work the inner thighs, outer thighs, and hips. In the first pose, your long-term goal is to be able to stand with straight legs separated 3-4 feet (94-122 cm) apart, folding forward from the hips with your spine in a neutral position to place your forehead on the floor between your feet. To maximize your opportunity to develop the necessary flexibility in the legs, hips, and lower back, keep your shoulders and chest squared up with your hips, and allow the forward pelvic rotation to be the movement that takes you to your edge.

STARTING POSITION: *move the mat to give a side-on view in the mirror; stand at the left end of the mat.*

SETTING UP Standing in Tadasana, inhale and take your arms overhead. Exhaling, step your right leg as far to the right as you comfortably can while bringing your arms down in line with your shoulders. Place your feet parallel, heels in line, and align your joints all the way up, ears over shoulders, chin neutral.

2 Fold forward

Exhale and begin folding forward from the hips (a pelvic rotation). Work with your breath and maintain the alignment in the upper and lower body. Inhale, drawing strength and space into the appropriate opposing areas. Exhale and stabilize, releasing any gripping and relaxing deeper into the pose.

Hot tips Hips behind your heels, legs angling back? You won't achieve a full calf stretch. To remedy this, bring your legs forward until your hips are directly above your ankles. Take your calves forward, thighs back until the knees are centered between the hip and ankle joints. If the hip and ankle joints are aligned but your knee pushes back, soften behind the knee and center it with the ankle and hip by taking your calf forward and thigh back. This stabilizes the knee in the center of these joints. Watch out also when the chest collapses and the upper spine rises above the curvature of the lower spine, which overstretches the upper spine. Work on opening the chest and pelvic diamonds (see page 23).

1 Stabilize

Inhaling, stabilize the legs (draw down through your feet and up through your legs, keeping both sides of the feet on the floor and outer ankles pulled in; bring the energy in the lower legs in and forward, the upper legs apart and back, joints stacked in a perpendicular line). Exhale and release any gripping without losing stability. Inhaling, stabilize the spine in a neutral position (create space in the front of the pelvis and chest, lift your pelvic floor, and relax the buttocks and shoulders). Inhale and acknowledge the stability in both areas.

3 Introduce the arms

Once your torso has rotated around your legs enough, reach back with your arms and grab your calves, ankles, or, depending on your flexibility, cup your hands beneath your heels. Apply a gentle pulling action to the stretch. Make sure your chest stays open and squared with the hips, your spine remains neutral. Inhale, drawing strength and space into the appropriate opposing areas. Exhale, stabilizing and relaxing any gripping and, as you release deeper into the pose, fold into the elbows. Draw through your elbow fold away from the center (this really opens the chest and stabilizes the upper spine as you fold in deeper at the groin crease). Lift up through the crease and move your body closer to your legs. Hold for 20 seconds.

WORKING THE POSE Once you can maintain a neutral spine and straight legs while folding your body into your legs, bring your chin away from your throat without crunching the back of the neck so the forehead rather than crown of the head sits between your feet.

COMING OUT Stabilize, then reverse the moves that took you into the pose. Inhaling, come up with a neutral spine and stable, strong legs. Exhaling, step your right leg to the left, arms back to your sides in Tadasana for two breaths. Repeat a second set.

TRIANGLE POSE

TRIKONASANA

A blend of several standing postures, known in traditional hatha yoga as the Extended Triangle (Utthita Trikonasana), Warrior II (*Virabhadrasana II*), and Extended Side Angle poses (Utthita Parsvakonasana), this position, with its external rotation of the legs and forward rotation of the pelvis, creates a stretch in the inner thighs as the hips open up. There are many opposing factors to bear in mind while you work, and it really puts your overall strength and hip flexibility to the test. Setting up the foundations well will equip you to overcome this pose's multiple obstacles, and will allow you to enjoy stretching into the angles, leaving you feeling as powerful as a warrior.

STARTING POSITION: *turn the mat lengthwise to the mirror so you see the front-view alignment; start at the left end of the mat facing the mirror.*

SETTING UP From Tadasana, inhale and bring your arms overhead. Exhale and step your right foot as far to the right as you can while bringing your arms down to shoulder-level, palms facing down. Turn your palms up, inhale, expand the width of your chest, and rotate your inner elbows up. Exhale and turn your palms down. Turn your right foot to a 12 o'clock position, your left foot to 10 o'clock. Inhaling, lift the inner part of your front knee and thigh, and rotate this leg outward. Exhale and draw your upper leg bone in and up under the hip, providing support for the body. Stretch the outer edge of your left foot into the floor while drawing the outer ankle in; stabilize the leg with the kneecap lifted.

Fold to the side

Keeping the inner knee of your front leg lifted and the thigh spiraling up under the hip, inhale and soften into the groin crease while bringing your right arm straight up over the shoulder, palm facing forward. Exhale and fold to the side, drawing in at the groin while reaching upward through your right arm to create a sideways "V" formation (>) with your right arm and torso and right leg. Align the left side of your torso with your left leg. Inhale while re-establishing your foundations, and soften into the right groin and back of the knee.

Exhaling, continue to draw into the fold of the groin and knee, sending the knee toward the heel and making the thigh parallel. The knee must never go beyond the ankle. If flexibility permits, slide your left heel back, deepening the angle formed at the groin.

Hot tips Front leg rotates internally with the knee in front of the ankle and hip? Back up and reestablish your foundations: lift your inner knee and thigh, and rotate the leg outward. Then draw the upper leg bone in and up beneath the hip for support. Stretch the outer edge of your left foot into the floor while drawing the outer ankle in, and stabilize the leg, kneecap lifted. If the toes of your back foot lift from the floor, keep the ball of that foot stretched wide into the floor; this also boosts stabilization.

2 Complete the triangle

Keeping the right shoulder up, swing the right arm like a pendulum to hang straight down. At the same time, bring your left arm up in a perpendicular line with shoulders and arms. Keep your right side over the thigh; firm your arms, right arm pressing back against the leg. Drop your head to align neck and spine. Turn the head left to align chin and shoulder; look at the thumb, as on page 80. Hold for 10 seconds: inhale into foundations and folds; exhale, stabilize; rotate torso and left leg away.

COMING OUT Inhaling, turn the head back to center, lift your right arm, and drop your left arm to bring your arms back to parallel while you straighten your right leg. Exhale, turn your left foot to a 12 'clock position, your right foot to 2 o'clock, and continue setting up to work on the left side. When finished on the left, turn the feet parallel and inhale the arms overhead. Exhale, bringing your right leg to meet the left and taking your arms to your sides. Take two breaths, before beginning a second set on both sides.

STANDING SEPARATE LEG HEAD-TO-KNEE POSE

DANDAYAMANA-
BIBHAKTAPADA-
JANUSHIRSASANA

This pose closes the hips and simultaneously lengthens the spine as you round your back and tuck your forehead above your knee (*sirsa* means head and *janu* knee). The internal rotation of the legs and forward rotation of the pelvis provide a stretch to the sides of the thighs and hips. To maximize the stretching of the posterior spine, make sure you first achieve a stretch in areas where the spine arches–the back of the neck and lower back. Then continue rounding to create a more even stretch along the entire length of the spine. This posture gives a deep contraction and compression to the throat and abdomen, which stimulates the organs and glands, especially the thyroid gland, whose hormonal secretions are responsible for regulating many of the body's physiological functions.

STARTING POSITION: *turn the mat back so that the top of the mat faces the mirror; stand at the left end of the mat, right side toward the mirror.*

SETTING UP From Tadasana, inhale, bringing your arms overhead and placing your palms together with thumbs crossed. Exhaling, step your right leg approximately 3 feet (91 cm) to the right. Pivoting on the balls of the feet, turn right to face the front of the mat and place your front foot parallel with the edge of the mat, leg straight. Turn your hips a few more times to the right as you bring your back heel around behind your left toes, stretching the ball of the foot into the floor while straightening your leg. Square up your torso toward the mirror. Without turning your left hip away, place your back heel down in line with your front heel, bending your front knee if necessary (in a lunge position).

Hot tips Legs not stable? Bend your front knee into a lunge, plant your foot firmly down, and stabilize the leg. Then straighten your back leg as you press through the ball of the foot to begin stretching the leg. Slowly stretch your heel to the ground.

WORKING THE POSE Continue to stretch your backside by evenly holding open the inner circle you have formed in connecting head to knee as you gently push your knee back with your head to straighten the front leg. Aim to take your hands in front of the foot, palms together in prayer position (as on page 84).

Hot tips Hips and/or shoulders not square? Veer to the side when bending forward? Change your foot position to give better alignment and stability. Also pay close attention when moving forward and curling in that your right and left sides are aligned.

When the chin is drawn back and up, the throat feels choked. Compressing and contracting the abdomen and chest makes it even more difficult to breathe. To be effective in the posture, surrender to the situation by remaining calm. Very slowly and gently bring the breath in as deeply as possible to areas of restriction, then slowly exhale, releasing deeper into the pose.

1 Round forward

Inhaling, internally rotate your legs and, back heel down, exhale and pivot the hips forward slightly, increasing the stretch to the back of the leg to a comfortable edge while stretching the buttocks. Inhale, draw chin to throat, then exhale, lifting into the throat while drawing into the groin crease. Inhale space into the back of the neck and pelvis, tuck the chin toward the base of the throat to hold the cervical stretch; at the same time, press the lower abdomen into the pelvis to hold the lumbar stretch. Exhale, drawing the torso back into the spine as you contract the abdomen and chest. Round forward evenly, right eyebrow above knee, nose aligned with inner thigh, hands either side of the front foot.

COMING OUT Inhale and untuck your chin. Exhaling, stretch forward and stabilize your spine and legs. Inhale and come up. As you exhale, pivot on the balls of the feet all the way to the left, facing the back of the mat. Repeat the pose. After coming up on an inhalation, exhale and pivot halfway to the right. Inhale, taking your arms overhead, and step your right leg to the left. Exhale your arms back to your sides. Take two full breaths before beginning a second set on both sides.

TREE POSE AND TOE STAND POSE

TADASANA VRKASANA–
PADANGUSTASANA

The stability of the mountain and tree (*tada* and *vrksa* in Sanskrit) are recalled in the final standing poses that challenge you to stand upright, stabilizing and balancing on one leg while you work on opening the hips, stretching the inside of the opposite leg into a half-lotus position (Tree Pose). The second set of this pose has an optional challenge–the Toe Stand. This is very hard on the knees if inflexibility is an issue for you, and is not recommended for students with any kind of knee injury, nor for beginners, who may not have the flexibility required to achieve this advanced level of control and steadiness.

STARTING POSITION: *standing in the center of the mat, facing the mirror.*

SETTING UP From Tadasana, release your weight from your right leg and rest the ball of your right foot on the floor beneath your right hip. Inhale and begin to fine-tune your standing alignment while relaxing behind the knee and in the crease at the groin.

1 Fold the leg

Exhale, stabilize, and bring your right thigh up parallel to the floor. Inhale, open up across the front of the hips and move your right leg away from center without allowing your hips to follow. Exhale and bring your right calf up to meet the back of your thigh. Inhale, stretching your toes evenly away from your ankle, keeping the outer part of the ankle drawn in. Exhaling, pivot slightly forward from the hips, reach down through your legs with palms facing forward, and grab the outside of your right ankle. Inhale and stretch your foot and knee back while drawing your sitting bone and ankle forward to allow the hip and inner leg to open to their maximum extent. Exhale and bring your knee in toward the center and back. Rest your right foot against the opposite thigh, eventually up in the crease of the groin, knees aligned. At the same time open up the front of your body, standing in balance as if in the basic standing pose for 10 seconds.

Hot tips Ankle sinks toward your thigh? Press the top of the foot toward the thigh and lift your ankle away, creating an opening along the entire length of the leg up to the hip.

Arching your back in order to stand upright? Instead, lift your folded knee, open your chest and pelvis, and stabilize before lowering the knee.

COMING OUT Stabilize, then lift your right leg, release the foot under the knee, and set the foot back down beneath the hip. Center yourself in Tadasana, then begin to work on your left side. After completing this side, take two breaths in Tadasana then set up for a second set on each side, starting on the right.

2 Optional Toe Stand (second set only)
To progress to the Toe Stand, at the end of step 1, fold forward evenly from the hips and place your hands on the floor. Look at the floor approximately 4 feet (122 cm) ahead (do not move your eyes; keep the head in a neutral position with the spine) as you rise up on the ball of the foot of the standing leg, then sit down just above the heel. Lift your body as you come up onto fingertips, drop your right leg to the level of the left leg, and draw them together. Draw in and up, bringing your body upright, lifting your hands into prayer position at chest level, as shown on page 88.

Hot tips You might like to try an intermediate position between steps 1 and 2 to help you toward the sitting toe stand. From the upright Tree Pose in step 1, fold forward, place your hands to the floor, and work with your breath to create the control you need to progress.

COMING OUT Place your hands back on the floor and raise your hips to straighten the standing leg. Stabilize; come up into upright Tree Pose. Release your folded leg, then repeat on the other leg. Stand still for two breaths. Lie back on the mat for two minutes.

WIND-REMOVING POSE

PAVANAMUKTASANA

After a brief two-minute rest in Savasana (see page 36), the first of the floor postures compresses the lower abdomen, stimulating the peristaltic action of the colon and therefore removing trapped gas (in the Sanskrit, *pavana* refers to breath, in this case air, and *mukta* means free from). The pose provides much the same stretch as the first standing balance (Standing Head-to-Knee, pages 60-63). Understanding the resemblance between these poses allows you to work a similar stretch using a different approach, increasing your awareness of the complete picture. Here, you do not have to struggle with balancing on one leg and so are able to move your focus to the obstacles found when you maintain the foundation of an open, squared-up torso. In so doing, you develop the flexibility for safe forward bending. There are three parts to each set in the stretch.

STARTING POSITION: *top of the mat toward the mirror; lying on your back with your head at the top of the mat.*

SETTING UP Lying on your back, extend your legs straight out from your hips with feet flexed, as if standing on the floor. Keeping your chest and pelvis open, ground down beneath your shoulder blades and hip bones to stabilize an open torso and prevent side bending.

Fold the right leg

Inhale space into the front of the body as you soften into the right side of the groin and knee-fold. Slide your right heel toward your right sitting bone while keeping the joints aligned and squared up. Flex your foot and toes, keep the outer ankle in, and press through the ball of the foot to maximize the stretch and equalize the stretching of both the inner and outer parts of the leg.

Exhaling, stabilize your torso while lifting your right foot off the floor, and place your hands, fingers interlaced, below your knee-cap. Soften into the folds of the knee, groin, and elbow as you fold your right leg into your body and bring your elbows to your sides. Work with your breath for 10 seconds as the compression stimulates the ascending colon. Release, reversing the folding action to extend the leg.

Hot tips Hip lifts toward the shoulder? Don't allow this to happen—it results in side bending and loss of foundation. Try anchoring your opposite shoulder down and back, then stretch diagonally into the lower part of the outer hip while bringing the leg in and up.

2 Fold the left leg

Reestablish your foundation: keeping your chest and pelvis open, ground down beneath your shoulder blades and hipbones to stabilize an open torso and prevent side bending. Repeat step 1 on the other side of the body, bringing your left leg in over your left side to compress and stimulate the descending colon.

Hot tips Foot, lower leg, and upper leg don't align when you fold one leg in? Keep the foundation in your body and move your foot away from center as you pull the outer part of your ankle in, squaring the foot with the lower leg. Soften behind the knee and groin, the width of the joint, then bring your lower leg in and upper leg out, aligning the legs so they fold in evenly behind the knee. Continue folding the leg over your lower abdomen without losing your foundation. The inner ankle and lower leg lengthen, as do the outer hip and upper leg.

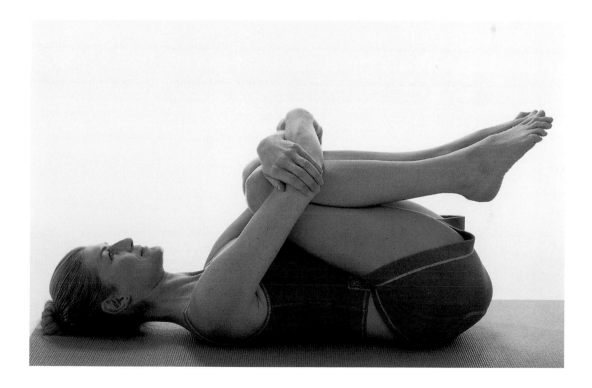

3 Bring both legs in

Reestablish your foundation and bring both heels toward your sitting bones. Inhale, opening the front of the body from the top of the shoulders to the groin creases. To increase your foundation points, stretch down into the groin creases while lifting your feet a few inches off the floor. Maintain this openness and, exhaling, bring your legs together and down over your lower abdomen. Inhale, and, lifting your spine into your thighs, rise up and wrap your arms around your folded legs, grabbing the opposite elbow if possible, as shown on page 95. If this is difficult, grasp the opposite forearm, wrist, or hand. Roll back, placing your upper back and head on the floor. Begin working with your breath to open the front of the body and allow the spine to move back in as the sides of the body begin to come to the floor. Ultimately, the back of the body rests evenly on the floor while you hold your folded legs against the lower part of your abdomen, a compression that stimulates the transverse colon. Work with your breath for 10 seconds.

Hot tips Don't close off the front of the body when lifting and wrapping the arms. Watch when pulling both legs in that your lower abdomen does not pull away from the thighs. This prevents the groin from exerting deep compression into the lower abdomen, and may overstretch segments of the lumbar (lower) spine.

COMING OUT Release your arms to your sides. Inhale, reestablish your initial foundation, and lift your thighs away from your body, bringing your feet down to the floor. Exhale, slide, or baby-step your heels away from your sitting bones to straighten the legs. Relax for two breaths in Savasana (see pages 36–37) before beginning a second set.

WORKING THE POSE If you are strong enough to maintain the foundation when exiting the pose, keep your heels slightly off the floor and move them away until the legs straighten; then set your legs to the floor. This requires more abdominal strength to stabilize the pelvis.

COBRA POSE

BHUJANGASANA

With this floor pose begins the spine-strengthening series of postures, which also prepare the body for backward bending. There are four postures: the first three isolate and strengthen a different segment of the spine, while the fourth works the entire spine. From the Sanskrit *bhujang,* meaning snake or serpent, the Cobra Pose focuses on strengthening the lower back. Additionally, it develops the back of the neck and thighs and opens the chest. These instructions are not for a full Cobra Pose, but a variation commonly referred to as Baby Cobra.

STARTING POSITION: *on hands and knees in the center of the mat, facing the mirror.*

SETTING UP From the hands and knees position, with the tops of your feet at the back end of the mat, bring the inner sides of your feet, ankles, knees, and thighs together. Place your hands forward on the mat, chest-width apart, and begin to relax the back of the body forward, bringing the thighs, pelvis, abdomen, and chest (in that order) down onto the mat. As your chest comes down, stretch back through the crease of the elbows and slide your palms back so that your hands and fingers sit directly beneath your shoulders. Make sure your fingertips are in line with the top of the shoulders, little fingers with the outside edge, chest resting between your hands. Bring your head down, ears in line with your shoulders, nose lightly touching the mat, to establish a neutral spine before beginning the pose.

1 Establish a foundation

Keeping the top of the feet, front of the pelvis, and abdomen on the floor, inhale, lifting your knees and navel up (engage the thighs and navel center) while drawing your tailbone down toward the pubis. Do not allow your ribs to lift from the floor. Exhale, stabilizing your foundation while relaxing your chest open.

Hot tips A sure sign of lack of foundation is the top of the feet and tailbone lifting from the floor, compressing the lower back. To remedy this, maintain contact with the floor from belly to toes while engaging the thighs and navel center.

2 Lift the upper body

Inhale, lifting the upper body (lower rib to top of head) away from the floor. Do not push away using your hands. Exhale and arch the upper back as you draw back through the elbow crease, shoulders, throat, and face. Move the upper part of the spine forward, stretching open across the chest. Keep your hands free from weight, shoulders down away from your ears, and chin in a neutral position, as shown on page 98. Work with your breath to create a solid foundation while opening the chest. Find your edge, hold, and breathe.

Hot tips Pressing your hands into the floor? Lifting your belly with your chest? Compressing the lumbar spine by arching? Lower your upper body and reestablish your foundation. Do not lift higher than the bottom of your ribs, nor any higher than you have the strength to hold. Draw back through the elbow crease to help remove weight from the hands.

COMING OUT On an exhalation, slowly lower your spine to the floor. Adopt the Prone Savasana position by turning your head to the right and placing your right ear where your nose was. Extend your arms along the sides of your body, palms up, and allow your legs to rotate internally, relaxing with toes in and heels out. Take two breaths and set up for a second set. At the end of the second set, relax again in Prone Savasana, this time with your left ear on the mat.

HALF-LOCUST POSE

SALABHASANA

The previous floor pose strengthened the lower spine while lifting and opening the upper body. This pose, named for *salabha*, the locust, does the opposite, strengthening the upper body while you lift and lengthen the lower body. Here, the arms are planted beneath the body, palms, wrists, and elbows open to the floor. In the beginning, this can prove the greatest challenge–it feels as if your arms might break –but it is actually beneficial for those with symptoms of carpal tunnel syndrome and tennis elbow. As the palms, wrists, and elbows stretch open, discomfort eases and you increase your focus on lifting into the pose. There are two parts to the pose. First, you lift one leg, then the other, the rest of the body stabilized on the floor. This stretches open the front of the pelvis, groin, and front of the legs. In the second part, you lift the pelvis and legs. The upper spine draws down into the chest; the lower body lightens and lifts. Visualize a seesaw: as you add weight to one end, the other end rises.

STARTING POSITION: *lying face down, head toward the mirror.*

SETTING UP Turn your head to rest your nose and the front of your chin lightly on the floor. Your arms stay at your sides, inner forearms and palms facing down. Inhale space into your chest, stretching from ribs to upper arms. Rotate your inner elbows down into the floor and spiral your upper arms away to open the shoulders. Exhale and relax the upper spine down, bringing your chest to rest on the floor between your arms. Keeping your chest open into the floor, inhale and lift into the groin crease as you walk your knees in beneath your hips to raise your abdomen and pelvis off the floor. Keep your palms open to the floor, middle fingers aligned with the center of the wrists.

Spread your fingers and thumbs apart, and slide your hands toward the center, bringing your little fingers to touch if possible. Lie your body on your arms, flattening them out as you stretch your legs straight back onto the floor. Do not roll your shoulders in beneath the chest to bring your arms under your body; the chest stays open wide between the arms, and the arms angle in to form a triangular base.

Hot tips Palms and forearms face up? Shoulders roll under your body and chest lifts from the floor? Review your setup. Some teachers advise the following maneuvre: roll up to one side and place that arm on the front of the body, palm up; then roll down and up to the other side to position the second arm; roll back down, lying on both arms. A tight chest is more likely to remain closed, however, when the arms are positioned in this way.

Elbows point out from your sides or won't straighten? Separate your hands enough to pull your inner elbows down into the floor, spiraling your upper arms away while drawing your chest down between your arms. Eventually work your hands back in, bringing your elbows beneath your body.

Lift alternate legs

Stabilize your torso to establish foundation– as your back relaxes down, gravity stretches your front open, arms straight. Keeping your torso square and slightly down, lift the right leg away from the floor, pelvis equally weighted right to left. Without pulling the leg away from the hip joint, straighten and square the right leg and foot: draw up from the knee, pull in the outer ankle, flex the toes, press out through the ball of the foot. Maintaining the stable torso and straight leg, inhale and internally rotate the thigh; exhale and lift the inside edge of the foot to raise the leg. Work breath by breath for three cycles, raising the leg as if placing the foot on the ceiling. Exhale, slowly lower. Relax the leg; repeat on the left.

2 Lift both legs

Adjust your upper body and arms, if necessary, and keep your face down toward the mat to avoid straining your neck. (Do not lift your head to look in the mirror.) Draw your navel toward your spine and keep your sides long from ribs to hips to stabilize the middle and lower back. Bring your legs together, pulling the outer ankles in so the inner ankles and feet touch, then straighten the legs, lifting your feet from the floor. Keep the legs level with the pelvis, the body stable from crown to toes, resting on your chest, forearms, and hands. Inhaling, press the back of your forearms and hands down, draw your upper spine down between your arms, and the top of your thighs toward the floor while lifting your pelvis away from your arms and hands. Focus on maintaining a stable line from lower ribs to toes; try to avoid collapsing into the lower spine.

WORKING THE POSE To work with the breath, inhale and draw down into your foundation–upper back, forearms, and hands–while stretching your pelvis evenly away from your ribs and up from your arms with straight legs. On each exhalation, relax your chest open to the floor and lengthen the front of your body in a straight line from ribs to toes. As the lift continues upward, begin to feel the weight come down into the center of your chest.

Hot tips Collapse into the lumbar spine when lifting both legs? This also happens when you try to lift the legs rather than the pelvis. In both cases, lower your legs and stabilize from ribs to toes in a straight line. (Lengthen between rib cage and pelvis, navel in, top of thighs down, top of feet up.)

COMING OUT Stabilize your foundation on an inhalation and slowly lower your body back down on the exhalation. Adopt the Prone Savasana position, turning your head to the right and relaxing for two complete breaths. Repeat a second set, then relax again in Prone Savasana, this time with your left ear on the mat.

FULL LOCUST POSE

POORNA-SALABHASANA

In Sanskrit, *poorna* means full, indicating a more intense Locust Pose that strengthens the middle part of the spine. Your aim is to hold your spine in neutral and your legs straight while trying to come up into a wide "V" shape. This requires you to lengthen both the upper and lower spine, and to stabilize in the middle where these two opposite curvatures meet–no mean feat. The lifting of the legs also stretches open the groin and strengthens the hamstrings. In a class, this pose is held for 10 seconds. Keep this length of time as your goal, bearing in mind that it may take some weeks or months of yoga practice to achieve the ideal.

STARTING POSITION: *lying face down, head toward the mirror*

SETTING UP Turn your head to bring your nose and the front of your chin to the mat. Extend your arms, palms facing down and back, approximately 6-8 inches (15-20 cm) from your hips. Stretch open the chest cavity with your breath, then exhale and relax the upper spine down, resting your chest on the floor. Do not allow your shoulders to round back down toward the floor. Bring your legs together, drawing the outer ankles in and touching the inside edge of the feet together. Firm up the legs and rotate them externally, then lift them slightly from the floor.

Next firm the arms, lifting them to shoulder-level and stabilizing. Then lift your face straight up from the floor to align and stabilize the neck in a neutral position. At the same time, draw your navel up toward your spine. With the joints in the ankles, knees, wrists, elbows, shoulders, and neck now stabilized, inhale, drawing into these stabilized areas and exhale, releasing any excess tension or gripping (including tension in the mind).

Hot tips When externally rotating your legs, feel your buttocks come together, firming the tailbone down toward the pubis. This is very important in stabilizing the spine. If the tailbone lifts, you compress the lumbosacral region, and any effort to go up comes from the lower back (see page 23).

1 Raise the thighs

Imagine your calves are heavy and, on an inhalation, lift your thighs to a comfortable edge. Keep your legs together and try to open the space at the back of the knees and front of the ankles–a sensation like opening your eyes wide. Exhale, stabilize the lift, and release excess tension.

Hot tips Knees bend and legs separate at the knees? Return to setting up and reestablish straight legs. In the beginning you may need to work with legs hip-width apart. To connect with the movement, practice lifting the legs only, imagining the calves are so heavy they cannot rise without the thighs.

2 Lift the upper body

Imagine the back of your head and upper back are heavy and, on an inhalation, lift the lower ribs up (not forward and up, just up away from the floor). Continue working with the breath, coming up evenly. Work to keep the head, hands, and feet at the same level, treating the entire body as two very stable pieces that "V" upward. Inhale to lift, and, on the exhalation, release unnecessary tension and gripping. Try to hold the pose for 10 seconds.

Hot tips Upper back arches? Lumbar spine collapses? Lower your head, chest, and arms. Stabilize this zone, keeping torso, head, and arms on the same plane; lift again. Imagine the head, arms, and upper back are so heavy they cannot rise above the abdomen and pelvis. Head and hands higher than feet? Bring the chest down until the head and arms are even with the feet. Continue lifting both ends equally.

COMING OUT To release, slowly lower both parts of the "V" to the floor on an exhalation. Adopt the Prone Savasana position, turning your head to the right and relaxing briefly. Repeat a second set, then relax again in Prone Savasana, this time with your left ear on the mat.

BOW POSE

DHANURASANA

Resembling a strung archer's bow in form (*dhanura* means bow), this floor pose manipulates every segment of the spine to create all the openings your body requires to achieve safe and comfortable backward bending. When performed correctly, the posture stretches the chest, groin, and thighs simultaneously. Aim to hold this pose for twice as long as the previous three spine-strengthening poses, building up slowly to the 20 seconds the asana is allotted within a classroom setting.

STARTING POSITION: *lying face down, head toward the mirror.*

Turn your head back to center, nose and front of chin toward the mat to keep your head and neck in the neutral position. Extending your arms down the sides of the body, palms downward, allow your inner elbows to relax toward the floor and your upper arms away. This rotation opens the chest and allows the upper spine to drop. Relax your spine down through the center of your body. Draw your outer ankles in and point your toes away from your knees to align each foot with its leg. Engage the thighs to stabilize the knee joints, then rotate the entire leg externally. This stabilizes the dropped sacrum–feel the front of the pelvis ground down toward the mat.

1 Establish a foundation

Fold in behind the knees and bring your heels toward your buttocks. Reach back and take hold of the outside edge of your feet, placing your palms on the sides of your feet, your fingers across the top of each foot. Flex your toes back toward your hands, then draw the ankles and lower legs in toward each other. Ideally, the legs stay hip-width and parallel, and eventually they touch. Kick your feet back to stretch your arms without lifting your body from the floor.

Lift up

2 Stabilize your spine down toward the floor and lift your knees. As your thighs begin to stretch upward, keep kicking back into your hands. Lift your face and chest upward, and arch the upper back by moving the spine forward into your chest. Continue working with the breath, forming an archer's bow with your body. Inhale space into your chest, groin, and thighs and, as you exhale, press down and stretch up. For full backbend stretching, your shoulders and knees must rise to the same level. Hold the pose for twice as long as the previous three poses–aim for 20 seconds. To avoid struggling as you hold, grow into the pose with each breath.

Hot tips Tailbone lifting the pelvis away from the floor, compressing the lower back? Release the pose enough to set the pelvis down, and begin again. Try to keep the area from groin to ribs down–take only the thighs, chest, and head up.

Knees lower than shoulders? You won't stretch evenly– the chest gets more of a stretch than the groin or thighs. Lower your chest and focus on lifting your knees. When the knees reach the height of the shoulder joint, begin again to work the stretch evenly.

Be careful not to let your head and neck hang forward. When arching the lower back, drop the chin slightly and lift up into the crease at the throat, behind the ears, and into the base of the skull. At the same time, relax your shoulders away from the ears. Now bring your face and shoulders back as the spine stretches forward into your chest.

COMING OUT Release on an exhalation and slowly lower your body, releasing your hands from your feet. Continue releasing the legs, chest, and arms down to the mat. Adopt the Prone Savasana position with your right ear down, and relax for two full breath cycles. Repeat a second set, and relax again in Prone Savasana, this time with your left ear on the mat.

FIXED FIRM POSE

SUPTA VAJRASANA

With this pose begins a series of four postures that alternate backward and forward bending to improve spinal flexibility. In Supta Vajrasana (*supta* means between and *vajra* fixed or firm), the lower body is prepared for bending backward as you sit with legs folded between the feet, then lie back with arms overhead, grasping opposite elbows. Your focus for Fixed Firm Pose is to stretch the front of the thighs and groin—a region often neglected during back bends. When these zones are tight, back-bending begins in the lumbar spine, creating compression to an area that naturally has less space. As you begin to rotate the pelvis back to bring the spine down to the floor, the stretch increases in the front of the leg between the knee and top of the pelvis. When performed correctly, the pose is great for rehabilitating the knees, but done incorrectly, it can create or exacerbate a knee problem. Props, such as a block or folded blanket, are very useful for those with extremely tight legs or injuries that prevent deep knee-bending.

STARTING POSITION: *kneeling at the front of mat, facing the mirror.*

SETTING UP From Prone Savasana, look down at the mat, place your hands beneath your shoulders, palms down, and turn the top of your feet down. As you press through your hands and knees, lift up your pelvis and stretch up and back through the groin crease, bringing your sitting bones back. Keep your chest, face, and palms down while lifting the arms. Take a breath or two, then lift your chest and move forward, coming onto hands and knees. Move your knees to the front edge of the mat.

Place your knees directly beneath your hips, ankles straight back from the knees, top of the feet flat. Begin to fold back at the knee joints, lowering your thighs onto your calves, and with a slight internal rotation of your folded legs, sit between your feet. The ankles and heels should touch the upper thigh: make sure there is no space between leg and hip. If you cannot sit between your feet, use a prop (see page 32).

Hot tips It's OK to let the upper legs open wider, but you must keep lower and upper legs touching. It's very bad for the knees to separate them. If this happens, come onto the knees and reposition the legs before folding at the knee. Try internally rotating and "V"ing out the legs to get down with lower and upper legs connected. As you gain flexibility, bring the legs in and rotate them externally, lower legs pulled into upper legs.

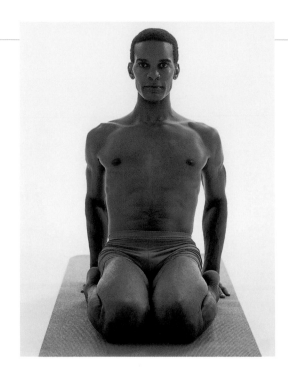

Begin to stretch

To stretch between the knees and top of the pelvis, place your palms on your feet, fingers toward toes. Begin to rotate the folded legs externally, turning the pelvis back. The buttocks slide underneath, the tailbone moves toward the knees, the top of the pelvis drops back toward the floor. Stretch back into the elbow creases, bending the arms and lowering right, then left elbows for support. Stabilize the spine and move the torso as one piece as far as possible. Eventually, the center of the buttocks rest on the floor when you lie back, as shown on page 116.

 Hot tips Spine arches away from the floor? Bring the head and shoulders up to a point at which you can neutralize the spine; go back down by rotating the pelvis. Keep working the stretch in the legs and pelvis. Don't begin bending in the lower back; this stops the thighs and pelvis from stretching, and stretches the lower abdominal muscles as the lumbar spine compresses.

2 Soften the spine
Once you are lying back, use your breath to neutralize the spine. Create a soft space in the lumbar and cervical regions: inhale, opening the chest and lengthening between the knees and hip crest; exhale, relaxing your back ribs, buttocks, and folded legs down to the floor.

3 Take the arms back
Bring your arms overhead without arching away from the floor. Place your hands on opposite elbows and relax as you lower the arms back into the floor. Breathe and enjoy. Aim to hold the pose for 10 seconds.

COMING OUT Come up just as you went down: bring your arms back to your sides and lift up on to the elbows, then the hands. Bringing the pelvis back over the tops of the legs, come up to sitting. Turn around and lie back in Savasana for two complete breaths. Sit up (see page 27) and turn around. Repeat a second set.

HALF-TORTOISE POSE

ARDHA-KURMASANA

You are required to sit with deeply folded legs in this floor pose. First, certain muscles in the legs have to stretch, then gravity assists you into position. Holding this folded-leg position isolates the stretch so that it becomes your foundation. Half-Tortoise Pose (*ardha* means half, *kurma* tortoise) is a forward bend with tightly folded legs, in which your focus should be on stretching the back of the thighs, buttocks, and lower back. You sit on the heels with legs and feet pulled together, arms extended overhead with hands in prayer position, and pelvis rotated forward to bring the spine over the thighs. The forehead and sides of the little fingers rest on the floor. It is important to stabilize the spine in a neutral position and to move the pelvis to bring it over the legs. This gives you maximum stretch in the areas that require it.

STARTING POSITION: *on hands and knees at the front of the mat, facing the mirror.*

Create a foundation

Inhale into the groin crease and feel your legs firm up, then draw your legs down to begin creating a foundation. As you exhale, stabilize the legs and begin to rotate your pelvis forward. Keep the front of your body open (creating a long, straight line between groin crease and top of the forehead) as you take your spine down over your legs (see forward bending, page 24).

SETTING UP On hands and knees, bring your legs together, heels touching, top of the feet down. Sit on your heels with an upright spine. Inhale and take your arms overhead, hands in prayer position with thumbs crossed. Exhale and relax the front of the thighs down to stabilize your body as you lengthen up, opening the front of the body and relaxing your shoulders over your hips.

Hot tips Unable to sit on your heels? Use a block, folded towel, or blanket to provide support.

2 Take the head down

Once your body is laid on top of your thighs, allow your head to come down, placing your nose and forehead on the mat. Then take the side of your hands down and draw your forearms in, straightening the wrists and elbows. Take the sides of the little fingers down and move your shoulders away from your ears. Try to hold the pose for 10 seconds, as in a class.

✱ Hot tips If, when coming down from the groin crease over the thighs, you find yourself closing the "V" without rounding forward, you might need to keep your arms at your sides until your chest and upper spine are down. At this point, bring your arms overhead, hands in prayer position with thumbs crossed, and finish setting up. When you release, you may need to take your arms to the side before coming up to sitting. As your strength and flexibility begin to balance, you will be able to take the arms back overhead.

WORKING THE POSE Use your breath in the pose to inhale space into the back of the thighs, buttocks, and lower back. Exhale down into the folds of the legs and relax the spine down into the front of the body.

COMING OUT To release, inhale, lifting the head, neck, and chest up enough to neutralize the spine. Exhale and stabilize the spine while lifting the sides of the little fingers off the mat. Inhaling, rotate the pelvis away from the thighs, bringing your spine upright with arms overhead. Exhale and take your arms down to your sides. Turn around and lie back in Savasana for two complete breaths, then do a Sit-Up (see page 27) and turn around. Repeat a second set.

CAMEL POSE

USTRASANA

The previous two floor postures comprised backward and forward bends in which movement was initiated in the lower portion of the torso, and your primary focus was the legs and hips. During the next two postures, movement begins in the upper portion of the torso, and your focus turns to the neck, chest, and abdomen. In Camel Pose you stand on your knees, arch your upper spine, reach back to grab the heels, and lift your spine to stretch open the chest. The throat and abdomen also benefit from the intense stretch.

STARTING POSITION: *kneeling at the front of the mat, facing the mirror.*

SETTING UP Kneel upright with legs hip-width apart: hips over knees; lower legs and feet (toes pointing away) directly behind the knees. Let the back of your lower legs and feet move toward the floor to form the foundation from which you rise up. Relax your tailbone down, and move the back of the thighs and buttocks forward as you stretch up the front of the legs to the top of the pelvis, stabilizing the legs and hips above the knee. Extend your arms down your sides, rotated so palms face forward.

1 Take back the palms

Inhale and lift your forearms, drawing back through your elbow creases to take your hands behind your hips. Drop your hands without moving your forearms, and place your palms on your buttocks, fingers pointing down, thumbs to the side. Exhale, stabilizing into your foundation as the front of your body lengthens from crown to knees.

✳ Hot tips Keep the body, including your head, upright when pulling your arms back; feel your spine begin to lengthen forward into your chest.

2 Bend back the upper spine

Inhaling, draw down into your foundation and hold the back of the body forward as you bring space with the breath into your front. At the same time, start bending back from beneath the shoulder blades, spine lifting into the chest and neck. The back of the head moves back and down with the upper spine (chin relaxed to the throat). Exhale, stabilizing the back. Form a long line from base of shoulder blades to back of knees as you lengthen your front over the supported arch. Lengthen the back of the neck, shoulders rolling away from ears.

3 Take hands to heels

Working with the breath, release your right palm from your buttock and move it back as you straighten the arm and reach down to your right heel. Cup the heel with your palm, thumb on the outside. Then lift along your right side, holding the heel, and release your left palm. Move it back and reach down for your left heel. Lift your spine as you pull on the heels, move your chin away from your throat, and allow your head to hang back from the neck. Work with the pose for 10 seconds.

Hot tips Can't reach back for the heels without collapsing the lower back? Keep hands on hips and work on developing the upper-back arch, using the arms for support. Press through the base of the palms while drawing back into the elbow creases to lift the base of the shoulder blades, taking the upper spine back and down. Bring chin to throat while lengthening the back of the neck to keep the head supported and stop the cervical spine from collapsing. Open the spine in the chest and back of neck before dropping the head.

WORKING THE POSE Open the chest with the breath by lifting and lengthening the upper spine into the strong arch. Inhale, draw the tailbone down, and anchor the lower legs, then lengthen the lower and middle spine up while expanding the chest. Exhale; lift upper spine into chest as you pull on the heels.

COMING OUT Come up the way you went down, with support. Inhale, lift up into the spine and release your right, then left hands to reach up for the hips. Continue lifting your spine up and forward to upright. Exhale your arms down to your sides, and sit back on your heels for one breath. Turn around and lie back in Savasana for two complete breaths. Perform a Sit-Up, turn around, and repeat a second set.

RABBIT POSE

SASANGASANA

This pose is another forward bend in which the spine is rounded with forehead on the knee (*sasa* means hare, or moon; *samga* closing or coming together). Here, you sit on the heels, tuck forehead to knees and lift the hips, rolling forward as if attempting a somersault while holding the heels until the arms extend fully, hips over knees. Your focus is continually to lift your spine through the abdomen and take the shoulders away from the ears to prevent head and neck compression. Rabbit Pose opens every posterior vertebral joint while stretching the sides, back of the neck, and lower back. Deep compression to the throat and upper abdomen stimulates glands and vital organs. As always, begin lengthening areas of the spine that naturally bend back, so the entire spine stretches without stressing those segments at which the curvature changes. In Rabbit Pose, this approach is even more important because of your change in foundation: when upside-down, it is all too easy to let gravity take you forward via the path of least resistance.

STARTING POSITION: *sitting on your heels at the front of the mat, facing the mirror.*

SETTING UP Sit up on your heels with heels together (draw the outer ankles in; stretch out through the big toes to pull the feet together). Keep your arms at your sides. Rotate your arms open and take them back toward your hips as you tilt forward from the hips. Inhale, bringing your chin into your throat without tilting your head forward or collapsing the chest. Exhale, tilting your head forward and lifting beneath the crease of the throat while taking the shoulders away from the ears. Inhaling, take the lower ribs back, lifting the abdomen in and up while pulling the tops of the thighs back to lengthen the lumbar spine.

Hot tips Unable to keep your heels together and the tops of your feet on the mat? Come onto your knees to reposition the feet. Place your knees so your thighs are parallel, lower legs aligned directly behind the knees. Straighten out each foot to align with the leg by pulling the ankle in while stretching in behind the inner knee crease as the toes extend evenly away from the knee. Place the top of each ankle and foot on the mat, then, without releasing the ankles, bring your legs together and sit down. Feel a slight internal rotation. Keeping the front of the ankle opened into the floor creates a strong foundation; without this anchor, you cannot lift the hips to roll forward with control. Most people habitually sit on the feet with toes in and heels out. This overstretches the outer ankle and foot and shortens the inner side, making full extension of the front of the ankle difficult.

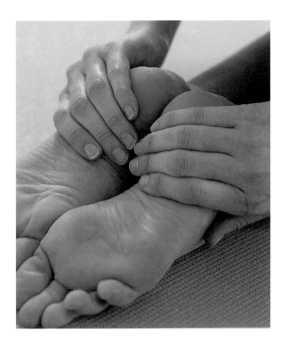

Forehead to knees
Contract your chest, rounding your upper back to kiss your forehead against your knees. As you are doing this, rotate your forearms to turn your palms toward the side of your heels, placing your fingers over the heels and your thumbs along the side of the foot to hold onto the feet. Hold the ankles in and keep pressing the tops of the feet and ankles down to provide your foundation.

2 Roll forward

Keeping your forehead kissing the knees and your hands on your feet, inhale, anchoring into your foundation and expanding the back of your body with the breath. Exhale, lift your hips, and roll forward until your arms are fully extended while lifting your shoulders and spine to keep weight from shifting forward onto your head. Ideally, the hips are directly above the knees, as shown on page 128. Continue to open up the inner circle you have formed against the backside of the body, creating a wheel shape. Work with the breath for 20 seconds.

Hot tips If you are unable to bend forward and reach your heels, perhaps because of your weight, use the instructions for the modified pose.

COMING OUT On an exhalation, lower your thighs down to your heels and release your chin from your throat. Inhaling, draw the front of the body back and up as you unroll, stacking the vertebrae to sit in an upright position. Take a breath here before turning around to lie back in Savasana for two complete breaths. Perform a Sit-Up, turn around, and repeat a second set.

Modified stretch

Start on hands and knees with legs together (ankles in, inner edges of feet touching, tops of feet and ankles open to the mat). Bring the thighs forward, hips over knees. Place the base of the palms under the shoulders, middle fingers centered, fingers wide; press down evenly. Keep the face parallel to the floor, shoulders away from ears. Fold the elbows, lower elbows behind wrists, bringing your forearms to the mat. Inhale the chin into the throat without tilting the head or collapsing the chest. Exhale, tilt the head forward, and lift beneath the crease of the throat while moving shoulders away from ears. Inhale the lower ribs toward the spine without rounding the upper back, and lift the abdomen in and up while stretching into the groin crease. Stabilize lower legs, ankles, and tops of feet down. As you bring sitting bones away from heels, contract chest, round upper back, and place crown between elbows. Lift into the throat and abdomen, moving shoulders away from ears by pressing the forearms. Maintain the foundation in the lower legs and forearms. To release, take chin from throat, and lengthen throat, chest, and pelvis. Press on the palms to lift the spine parallel to the floor as the elbows straighten. Lower sitting bones to heels; walk the hands back to sit upright.

HEAD-TO-KNEE POSE WITH STRETCHING POSE

JANUSHIRASANA &
PASCHIMOTTHANASANA

The penultimate floor pose has three parts and offers a wonderful combination of stretches. In the first two parts, forward bends with a spinal twist lead to rounding of the upper spine and stretching of the back of the legs. The third part comprises a full forward bend like the last part of Half-Moon Pose (pages 48-49), that weds spinal extension with a stretch to the back of the legs. In the Sanskrit, *paschima* means west, *ut* intense, and *tan* extension–this is an intense stretch for the west side (back of the body). You start the pose with legs in a "V" shape, then rotate rib cage and shoulders toward the thigh, bend the knee, and flex the spine to place forehead to knee. Your focus is straightening the leg as the upper spine rotates and flexes. In the third move, aim to extend the spine fully and straighten the legs as the torso eventually connects to the front of the legs. Because most back injuries occur as a result of improper deep forward bending and twisting, take time to understand the body mechanics of the pose.

STARTING POSITION: *sitting at the center of the mat, facing the mirror.*

SETTING UP Open your legs to create a "V" (a 60° angle). Place your hands back toward your hips, fingers spread and pointing away, thumbs beneath hips at the groin crease. Tilt your pelvis, bringing your body forward slightly over your thighs. Pressing down with fingers and thumbs, straighten your elbows, lifting through your chest, and lightening the pelvis away from the legs. At the same time, point the toes to firm the legs and internally rotate the legs to free the pelvis. Set your legs down and bring your pelvis and body upright, tall on the sitting bones. Refirm the legs, and rotate back to center, flexing feet and toes, knees and feet pointing up, spine rising out of the pelvis.

Bring your left knee up, heel sliding to sitting bone, calf pressing into thigh. Place your hands, fingers interlaced, below the knee, inhale, and stretch into the groin crease, elbow folds, and ball of the foot as your chest and knee crease rise. Exhale and anchor the left sitting bone as you relax the back of the thigh and hip down to solidify the foundation. Slide the outside edge of the left foot toward center (foot and toes flexed) to drop the folded leg left. When the knee is almost down, keep the toes flexed and extend the ankle. To do this, point away foot, then toes to place the outside edge of the top of the foot and leg down. Bring the folded leg in close and flat (ideally, heel against body in

the center). Bring your left big toe toward the shin as you slide your right leg over so left sole touches right inner thigh. Right leg and foot are squared, toes and foot flexed, foot and knee straight up.

Sitting tall, extend the arms, open the palms, and spread fingers and thumbs wide. Bring the arms back toward your sides, rotating externally so palms and inner elbows face out. While inhaling, press down the legs and shoulders and rise from hipbones to chest as you lift the forearms to take your arms overhead. Exhale, pull the elbows in, and relax shoulders away from ears as you stabilize your foundation.

Inhale (toes and foot flexed), lift behind your right knee, and slide your right heel as far as possible toward the sitting bone without losing your foundation (sitting bones, left inner thigh, right heel). Exhale and stabilize.

Hot tips Can't sit on the sitting bones with pelvis tucked under? Place a prop beneath them (see page 32). While sitting tall, reach back and pull loose flesh out from beneath the sitting bones. When dropping the folded leg, support the outer ankle with your left hand as the knee comes down. Then inhale, lift the outer ankle and sitting bone into the body; exhale, and relax the inner leg. Feel the leg release down on the mat. Throughout the movement be aware of your foundation.

1 Rotate to the right

Carefully rotate your rib cage away from your left side so your chest and shoulders turn toward your right thigh. Inhale, lengthening your sides as you ground into your foundation and your spine rises through the center. Exhale, looking forward, and rotate the rib cage only to the right. Take several breaths to rotate chest and shoulders, learning to isolate the move. When the chest is centered with the thigh, turn your head right to look over the knee. Inhale, bring your chin into your throat, and lift under the ears and into the base of the skull as the head tilts, moving shoulders away from ears. Place forehead on knee and reach out, interlacing the hands behind the ball of the foot. Exhale into your sitting bones, up through the lower abdomen, and release into the upper-body twist. Inhale into your foundation, rising up under the ribs. Exhale, rotate your upper body, and slide heel away from sitting bone, hands interlaced behind the foot, forehead on knee.

Work with the breath until your leg is fully extended. Aim to work each segment of pose for 10 seconds.

To release, let the foot go, release the chin, bring your upper body up, and twist back to center. Pause to inhale and exhale, then release the left leg back to the "V" formation.

Hot tips When rotating the rib cage, look forward to help isolate the move; watch in the mirror to see what you feel and resist any movement not consistent with your goal. The body typically follows the eyes; since you don't want anything below the ribs to follow, pay close attention to your intention.

WORKING THE POSE For advanced students, stretch into the elbow folds, bring the elbows down to the mat next to each calf, and lift your right heel from the floor.

2 Work the left side
Begin the setup again, this time with right leg folded in, then reverse the directions for step 1 to stretch the other side of the body.

3 Connect trunk and thighs
Lie back and perform a quick Sit-Up. Turn sideways, profile in the mirror. Walk your legs back to sit on your sitting bones, and pull away loose flesh. Firm the legs; flex feet and toes. Bring the legs together and rotate them internally to touch. Lifting behind the knees and scooting heels toward sitting bones, stretch the hipbones, lower ribs, and chest up the front of your legs, closing gaps from the groin crease up.

Reach forward and place first and second fingers between first and second toes; place your thumb on top of the big toe and wrap the fingers around. Draw back through the elbow creases, open the chest, and move shoulders and head back to align yourself from crown to tailbone. Inhale into the groin and ankle creases as spine and back thighs rise up into each other. Keep ears over shoulders, shoulders away from ears. Exhaling, anchor into your foundation (sitting bones and heels) as you slide the heels forward to straighten your legs. Work with the breath until your legs are extended to the point at which you can no longer maintain both the spinal extension and connection with the thighs.

At this point, exhaling, lower the knees and bring the torso up in one piece, straightening your arms as you pull back the toes, feet fully flexed. Torso and legs form a "V." Work

with your breath, keeping your legs firm as you continue to extend the spine over them. As you inhale, rotate the legs internally while rotating the pelvis forward and, starting at the back of the pelvis, pull your spine up and open across the width of the chest. On the exhalation, stretch forward through the ankle creases and stretch back into the crease of the groin and elbows, folding the body in half.

Hot tips Maintain full connection of legs and torso as in the fourth step of Half-Moon Pose (see pages 48-49). Trying to pull a rounded back over the legs is physically impossible and harmful (see page 28). Difficult to maintain even foot flexion? Outside edge of the foot stretches away? Instead of holding the big toes, place your hands on the sides of the feet to help work through inflexibilities and weaknesses in the sides of the legs and feet. Make sure to pull the outer ankle in. If your legs are straight, soften behind the knees with a slight bend, point the foot and flex the toes, keeping feet square with legs, then flex the feet.

COMING OUT Let go of your toes and lift up behind the knees, sliding your heels back while bringing your spine upright. Pause to inhale and exhale, turn around and lie back in Savasana for two complete breaths. Perform a Sit-Up, turn around, and repeat a second set.

SPINE TWISTING POSE

ARDHA-MATSYENDRASANA

You have reached the final floor pose of the hot yoga series: the last exercise in the series consists of cleansing work with the breath. Spinal twisting is a neutralizing move in which you work diagonally with the right and left sides of the spine. It also provides a nice massage for the internal vital organs. In this pose you remain seated with legs folded and crossed, spine upright and twisting from the bottom of the rib cage up to the skull to bring the knees and shoulders into a single line. The hips and shoulders should remain level and the spine upright. On releasing, you experience an intense sensation of refreshment, both physical and mental.

STARTING POSITION: *sitting at the center of the mat, facing the mirror.*

SETTING UP Sit on your sitting bones with knees bent, soles of the feet on the floor. Inhale down into your sitting bones and heels to ground the body, and on the exhalation rise up beneath the crease at the knees and underarms, relaxing the groin crease and shoulders down. Keep your ears over your shoulders, eyes looking forward.

1 Arrange the legs

Slide your left foot up beneath your right thigh, pointing the toes evenly away from your knee to keep the ankle straight as you place the outside of the leg on the mat, heel next to the outside of the right sitting bone. Inhale into the sitting bones again, and, exhaling, rise up to lengthen both sides of your torso. Place your right leg over your left, heel by the top of the left knee. Keep both sitting bones on the mat to level the pelvis. There should be a straight line from left to right toes (left toes, heel, lower leg, knee, right heel, toes.)

Hot tips Unable to sit on both sitting bones with pelvis and shoulders level and both sides of the body equal in length? Keep your bottom leg straight and place your left heel in front of your right sitting bone with the leg straight. Bend your right leg, placing the heel on the outer side of the left knee in front of the left sitting bone. Alternatively, use props to level your hips and shoulders (see page 32). Place something beneath the sitting bone on the mat to bring it to the same level as the other. When you ground down into the prop, the other hip counterbalances, allowing a stretch down your higher side.

2 Twist the spine

With arms extended down, straighten from fingertips to shoulder, then rotate, palms facing up. Inhale, stretching down into the fold at the groin as the front of your torso rises and opens across the chest. Bring your right lower side and thigh into each other, your shoulders and ears away from each other. Exhale and stabilize, keeping your right lower side (below the ribs) into the thigh, your head facing forward. Then twist your rib cage and shoulders to take the left side of the ribs to the right thigh. Keep working with your breath to rotate the chest, bringing the shoulders in line with the knee. Place the back side of your left arm on the outside of the right lower leg, then rotate the forearm to place the palm on the left knee. Rotate the right forearm to turn the palm to face left, lift up into the crease of the right elbow, then take the folded arm behind you. With the elbow below the shoulder and the forearm against the body, reach around with the hand to place the palm on the left thigh.

3 Work with the breath

Once the spinal twist is set up, bring your chin around to your right shoulder, keeping it parallel to the floor, and look to the right. Work with the breath. Inhale down into your sitting bones, and rise up through your center, opening the front of the body; on the exhalation stabilize and twist your chest, shoulders, neck, chin, and eyes, looking all the way to the right.

Modified stretches

If you cannot twist enough to place your left arm over your left leg without collapsing in the chest, lift your forearm, folding in at the elbow, and place the palm on your right knee, keeping the elbow down. Stretch into the crease of the elbow when you inhale into the groin crease.

If you are unable to reach your right arm around your back without collapsing the chest, place your palm on the floor by your hip, fingers pointing away, as shown on page 140. Press into the floor through the base of the palm when you inhale.

COMING OUT On an exhalation, turn your head back, release your right then left arms, and bring your chest back around past center to countertwist gently to the left before resting back to center. Release your legs and set up again, reversing the instructions to work on your left side.

BLOWING IN FIRM (HERO) POSE

KAPALBHATI & VAJRASANA

Hot yoga begins and ends with pranayama, breathwork. At the start of the series, it opened the lung tissue, allowing more vital life-force to enter the body. This final pranayama is cleansing, removing excess carbon dioxide–a by-product of metabolism. It is performed sitting in Vajrasana, Hero Pose. The breath is an exhalation only–the abdomen contracts in and up, forcing air up and out. Inhalation comes automatically as a response to the release of the abdominal contraction, drawing air naturally back into the lungs. Although in hatha yoga this type of breathing is frequently taught through the nostrils, in hot yoga, you work 100% through the mouth. It is also known as "skull shining" (*kapala* means skull): feel the breath come up and behind the roof of the mouth and out through the nostrils, shining the skull. The action is heat producing and stimulating, burning off and clearing mind and body of congestion or stagnation.

STARTING POSITION: *sitting at the center of the mat.*

SETTING UP With legs together and folded, sit upright on your heels. Keep your spine upright so the joints stack: ankles beneath hips beneath shoulders, ears over shoulders. The abdomen is long, chest open, shoulders relaxed, chin parallel to the floor. Straighten your arms in front of your chest, shoulder-width apart with palms facing, and rotate them externally to set the chest in the open position. Then turn your palms down by rotating at the wrists, and set your straight arms on your thighs. Extend the arms fully, resting palms above the knee on the thighs.

Hot tips Can't sit comfortably on your heels? Place a prop such as a folded blanket beneath your sitting bones to relieve pressure on the knees (see page 32). If you can't sit comfortably with heels together because the front of the ankle is tight, place a rolled towel or the rolled end of the mat beneath your ankles.
Spine rounds forward when your arms are straight? Relax into the elbow creases and slide your palms up the thighs as you lengthen your belly and open your chest. Let your elbows hang below your shoulders as you hold the spine upright.

Begin the breath
Smoothly inhale and exhale completely, relaxing the mind and any gripping tension used to hold the body in position. Contract your lips in front of your teeth as if blowing up a balloon, then draw your abdomen deeply inward and up along the spine as you make a "SHHH" sound. At the end of the sound relax your abdomen and feel the breath come back naturally into your body. Repeat for a total of 60 counts. After finishing the first set, take a full, deep inhalation and exhale completely.

Hot tips Relaxation is the key to moving the air in and out effectively and comfortably.

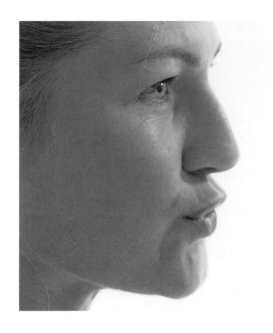

Hot tips Practice slowly and methodically until you achieve the feeling of a strong abdominal contraction and full emptying of the lungs followed by an abdominal relaxation and natural filling of the lungs.

COMING OUT When you are ready, rise up and turn around to lie on your back for the final Savasana.

2 Perform a second set

Begin a second set, making it faster this time, while retaining the same intensity of abdominal contraction. At the end of the second set, seal your practice by taking a slow, full inhalation, then make a fist with your right hand and place it at your navel, covering it with the palm of your left hand. Exhale very softly and slowly as you fold over from the hips, placing your forehead in front of your knees. Continue the very slow release of breath and body until you reach a point of stillness, and enjoy the open space you feel inside.

THE COOL-DOWN

To get the most out of a yoga routine, follow strenuous work on poses with these simple cool-down techniques, designed to relax mind and body and bring you back down to earth, physically and mentally. The final Savasana the finishing touch to your routine–is one of the most important poses to follow any yoga practice. It is not unusual to drift away or briefly doze off in this posture as this is the first time you close your eyes in a pose. During the period you spend in the pose, the body is able to receive the full benefits of the time you just invested in yourself. As you completely relax, circulation flows freely into areas you have now awakened, bringing vital nourishment to cells once made stagnant by inactivity. It also gives the body a chance to transform newly created energy into stored energy for future use. The final Savasana offers the body and mind an opportunity to incorporate the new feeling of awareness you have experienced; it allows time for new patterns to become part of your physical and mental memory. For maximum benefit, please allow yourself at least five minutes to enjoy just being.

SAVASANA

FINAL DEAD BODY POSE

SAVASANA

Savasana (from the Sanskrit sava, meaning corpse) is one of the principal asanas in yoga. Its essence is relaxation, which relieves fatigue and promotes peace of mind. When you enter Savasana between postures in a hot yoga class, you try to get to the optimum position quickly, but during this final Savasana, take time really to establish the best possible alignment to enhance the pose. There are many ways to appreciate this asana, and they vary with the props available to you and the time allotted. Instructions follow for probably the most common basic position taught in a Bikram Method setting. In class, always lie in Savasana with your feet away from the front of the room or mirrors. A very senior teacher once told me that not pointing your feet toward the teacher served as a mark of respect. You may be your own teacher, so let it become a habit to turn around, head nearest the mirror, and let your highest point reflect back at you.

STARTING POSITION: *top of the mat toward the mirror; lying with feet away from the mirror.*

SETTING UP Begin by lying back on your mat. Extend your arms on the floor at your sides, and place your feet under your knees.

1 Release the torso

Inhale and lift your hips and ribs. Begin to rotate the arms externally while rolling the shoulders back, then draw your shoulder blades together and down the spine. Exhale, and slowly lower your ribs one by one to the floor. The diamond space between your throat, navel, and nipple line should feel open and relaxed. Just before your buttocks touch the floor, inhale and adjust your pelvis so that your belly and pelvic center are aligned with the floor. If a full teacup were placed in the center of your pelvic diamond (made by your navel, pubis, and front hipbones), it would not spill. Exhale and set your buttocks on the floor without tilting; feel openness as you relax this area.

2 Relax the legs

Inhaling, slide your heels away and, pointing your toes evenly away from your ankles, gently stretch your legs. Exhaling, allow your legs gently to rotate away from the center, hip socket to toes, and relax.

3 Position the head

Inhale and lift your head while keeping your shoulders in position; tuck your chin into your throat. Keep your chin tucked in as you replace the back of your head (prominent part of the skull). Exhale, allow the chin to lift to neutral, and bring your face parallel to the floor. Your chin and forehead should be almost level.

Hot tips Head drops back with the chin up high? Place a folded towel beneath your head to align your head and neck with the rest of your spine.

4 Turn inward

Softly close your eyelids and turn your gaze upward and inward. Bring your attention to your breath as you begin to scan your body. As you inhale, turn inward and gently expand while gathering any unwanted sensations or thoughts, then gently exhale and release them. Try to synchronize the movement of your breath with your desired intention to relax and release, and feel the results. Let your mind direct the action, and note the sensation as you synchronize thoughts, feelings, and actions into one-pointed mindfulness on the breath. You might find that the ideas on page 37 help you sink into this relaxation and reenergizing of body, mind, and spirit.

COMING TO When ready to get up, keep your eyes closed and slowly wiggle your fingers and toes. Gently stretch your skin with soft, full breaths. Inhaling, draw your knees to your chest and right arm overhead. Exhale and roll to the right, using the upper right arm as a pillow, stacking shoulders, hips, and legs. Extend your left arm over your left hip for support. Lie here for a few breaths. Try to feel the breath as it travels in and out through the back of your nostrils.

Hot tips Lying on your right side promotes left-nostril dominance, which encourages relaxation. Adopt the coming-to position—a good quick relaxation—when you really can't give yourself adequate time in Savasana. But try not to make a habit of it.

RESOURCES

Finding a class
www.yogafinders.com
www.self-realization.com/yoga
Two extensive yoga directories on
the Internet. Choose your
preferred style of yoga and
location.

Yoga Alliance Registry
122 W. Lancaster Avenue
Suite 204
Reading, PA 19607-1874
Tel: (888) 964-2255
(610) 777-7793
E-mail: info@yogaalliance.org
www.YogaAlliance.com
Choose from the style of class you
prefer and then find a location that
suits you.

Bikram Yoga College of India
World Headquarters
1862 South La Cienega Boulevard
Los Angeles, CA 90035
Tel: (310) 854-5800
E-mail: info@bikramyoga.com
www.bikramyoga.com
Go to the class-finder page and
look under Yoga College of India
Studios and Bikram Method
Instructors.

United States Yoga Association
2159 Filbert Street
San Francisco, CA 94123
Tel: (415) 931-9642
www.usyoga.org

Yoga Connection Tribeca
145 Chamber Street
New York, NY 10007
Tel: (212) 945-9642
www.yogaconnectionnyc.com
The school where Marilyn Barnett
teaches, and the first school in
New York City to teach Bikram
Method yoga.

Tony Sanchez
United States Yoga Association
2159 Filbert Street
San Francisco, CA 94123
Tel: (415) 931-9642
www.usyoga.org

Jimmy Barkan
Yoga with Jimmy Barkan
1119 North Federal Highway
Fort Lauderdale, FL 33304
Tel: (954) 563-0488
www.jimmyyoga.com

Baron Baptiste
The Baptiste Power Yoga Institute
139 Columbus Avenue
Boston, MA 012140
Tel: (617) 441-2144
www.baronbaptiste.com

GLOSSARY

Abduction Moving away from the center of the body, or moving apart.

Adduction Bringing in toward center or across center, or bringing together.

Distal joints Pertaining to the joints away from center.

Extension Opening at the joint and lengthening.

External rotation Turning away from the front of the body.

Flexion Bending at the joint and closing.

Full rotation Circling.

Internal rotation Turning toward the front of the body.

Neuroglandular Relating to nervous and glandular tissue. Reconditioning, by optimizing regulatory communication and function between the two systems.

Neuromuscular Relating to nervous and muscle tissue. Reconditioning, by optimizing communication and function between the two systems.

THE POSES

ENGLISH	SANSKRIT
Standing deep breathing	Pranayama
Half-moon pose	Ardha chandrasana
Hands-to-feet pose	Padahastasana
Awkward pose	Utkatasana
Eagle pose	Garudasana (Bikram spelling: Garuasana)
Standing head-to-knee pose	Dandayamana-janushirasana
Standing bow pulling pose	Dandayamana-dhanurasana
Balancing stick	Tuladandasana
Standing separate leg stretching pose	Dandayamana-bibhaktapada-paschimot-thanasana
Triangle Pose	Trikonasana (Bikram spelling: Trikanasana)
Tree pose	Tadasana vrksasana
Toe stand pose	Padangustasana
Wind-removing pose	Pavanamuktasana
Cobra pose	Bhujangasana
Half-locust pose	Salabhasana
Full locust pose	Poorna-salabhasana
Bow pose	Dhanurasana
Fixed firm pose	Supta vajrasana
Half-tortoise pose	Ardha-kurmasana
Camel pose	Ustrasana
Rabbit pose	Sasangasana
Head-to-knee pose	Janushirasana
Stretching pose	Paschimotthanasana
Spine twisting pose	Ardha-matsyendrasana
Blowing in firm (hero) pose	Kapalbhati in vajrasana
Dead body pose	Savasana

ASANAS

INDEX

Page numbers in *italics* refer to captions